I0140359

Memoirs of a

Phenomenal Woman

Phenomenal Woman
Empowerment Alliance

Compiled by Lady Elder Bessie Sims

Published by Destiny House Publishing, LLC
Detroit, MI 48219

The Memoirs of A Phenomenal Woman

Published by Destiny House Publishing, LLC
Detroit, MI

International Standard Book Number:

ISBN-13: 978-1936867028
ISBN-10: 1936867028

Unless otherwise stated, all scripture quotations are from the Holy Bible, King James Version. Scripture references that do not have the Bible version noted are the author's paraphrase.

Original printing 2011
Cover design and Publication Layout: Destiny House Publishing, LLC
Photo: Dreamstime

Editing: Destiny House Publishing, LLC

For information:
www.destinyhousepublishing.com

P.O. Box 19774 Detroit, MI 48219
888.890.9455
Printed in the United States of America

FORWARD

Forward by Dr. Inecir Matthis

Lady Elder Bessie Sims is a spiritual giant and trailblazer in presenting us with this masterfully woven anthology of women for such a time as this! The veils of hidden assignments of assassination have been lifted as these women share and reveal their heartaches, struggles, and pains through life.

You will be moved and compelled by these women who display spiritual braveness and holy boldness as they lead you into their depths and history of despair, darkness and chaos. This reading encounter will cause you to embrace, understand and identify with every woman while sharing their pain, and rejoicing in their triumphs.

This page turner will be your spiritual journey to deliverance as you read and hear the heart of women just like you, speak to the very depths of your pain, to show you the way out.

Those that share their healing will cause you to emerge from your own cocoon stage and receive the transformation of healing into the spiritual butterfly you were meant to be.

Many of you will obtain the key and strategy to becoming a victorious overcomer of the assignments that have held you in spiritual, mental, emotional and physical bondage.

As you read her story, which is just like your story, you will understand your own needs and desire for the presence of God in your life and to close the gaps of bitterness and unforgiveness with the bridge of love.

You will experience the intricate handiwork of God as you see the assignments of pain, sorrow and despair broken as they become the iron sharpening your spiritual iron leading you into the very purpose for which you were destined!

For every individual born with a "Purpose" from God....the adversary (Satan) attaches an assignment of assassination for that "very" purpose. However, we have been given the Victory of Deliverance through Jesus Christ......

Pastor Inecir Matthis, Th.D

Victory of Deliverance Ministries

Author of: Stories of Transformation

Purposeful Living

INTRODUCTION

"Anyone can give up, it's the easiest thing in the world to do. But to hold it together when everyone else would understand if you fell apart, that's true strength." ~Unknown~

The message of this book is restoration and it is birthed from the lives of women who endured hardship as a good soldier and they decided that they were not going to give up. While walking through life, they were in bondage by the enemy and everyone gave up on them but as they began to look to the Lord He delivered them. As you walk through these pages of life, you will be amazed by the chronicles of each of the women who dared not to give up in times of trouble, great hurt and disappointment. Their testimonies will bless you. You will find that you have felt this, been in their shoes or lived their lives yourself. Some memoirs you will read and you might smile, laugh and even cry but most importantly you will remember how God brought you out. While looking in the face of overwhelming situations spelled out in these pages of life, these memoirs, you will find they didn't give up and therefore neither should you.

It is my prayer that as you read these entries you will discover yourself in these pages and say, "I am stronger, wiser and better".

God is a master at fixing any disaster and He wants to restore you back to your rightful place. And He wants to restore every area of our lives and make them even better than before. So just as he told the man in Mark 5:19-20 after He delivered him,

"***Go home to your own [family and relatives and friends] and bring back word to them of how much the Lord has done for you, and [how He has] had sympathy for you and mercy on you. And he departed and began to publicly proclaim in Decapolis [the region***

of the ten cities] how much Jesus had done for him, and all the people were astonished and marveled."

So today Memoirs of a Phenomenal Woman Anthology is making history and fulfilling the commandment that Jesus gave to a man he restored years ago. He told that man that was bond by the enemy, just as He has told these women "GO" back and deliver your family with this message of hope, that you too can be restored!! It doesn't matter how far you think you are out there or how much you have done. It doesn't matter if others have given up on you. Today the Lord has come to your grave site to deliver you from the bondage of the enemy. As you begin to read these chapters when you get to the one that blesses you, cry out to the Lord and he will heal you deliver you, set you free and restore you back to your rightful place in the kingdom. In Mark 5:6 before Jesus got close the man ran to Jesus and began to Worship Him. He cried out to Him before he was delivered because he knew restoration for his soul just step into his lonely, dark, hopeless, situation. Through these pages of life you will feel the every presences of the Lord step into your situation, right were you are, and when you feel Him - that tear, pattering of the heart, palms sweating just start worshipping because that is His glory resting on you to restore and set you free. When you feel the presence of God step into the room with you lift your hand and began to worship and say, deliver me oh Lord from the bondage of my past that is trying to choke out my future, my destiny my calling. And when you to do I declare that peace, joy and restoration will invade your life as you worship. And I promise, you will not be the same. And now I pray that after you have been restored that the God of all peace will send you to a place where you can worship in the beauty of holiness.

New Hope Worship Center and Phenomenal Woman Empowerment Alliance will always be in prayer for you as readers!! If need to contact us for prayer and connection to the Kingdom contact us through our websites: www.nhwcministry.org or www.phenomenalwomanalliance.org Forward: Dr. Inecir Matthis

-TABLE OF CONTENTS-

<u>"Who Am I" Phenomenal Woman</u>

By: Lady Elder Bessie Sims

A Phenomenal Woman

I Am A Woman Phenomenally!!

I defied the odds;

I soar above life's issues

I made my enemy my footstool;

I allowed wisdom and grace to lead me and now I walk in Victory!

Now God can use me to make a real impact in the lives of others!

I Am A Woman, Phenomenally!!

MEMOIR I

AMANDA'S MEMOIR AS A CHILD

"...This sickness is not unto death, but for the glory of God, that the Son of God might be glorified thereby." John 11:4 KJV

As a child I could remember being in the 5th grade wanting to go on a field trip to the county fair with my class. There was only enough room on the bus for 5 students and 3 alternates (back up students for the students that were chosen) from each class. I was selected to be an alternate. I could remember coming home excited because I was chosen as an alternate, telling my mom to make my lunch and get my clothes ready because I was going to the County Fair. Although I was just a back up for a student, I had faith that somehow I would be going on this trip. I could remember praying the night before the trip asking God to make it possible for me to go .....My prayer was God if you allow me to go on this trip, I will give you my heart, and not knowing this was part of the sinner's prayer. I was raised to say the "Our father" prayer at night, and sometimes my mother would quote scriptures like psalms 23, 91, or 27 but my siblings and I were not raised in the church. So where did I get this idea of offering my heart to God? I still don't know.

I believe God was dealing with me at a young age because I have always had that no matter what Faith. On the morning of the field trip, I went to school as usual with my lunch pack all dressed and ready to go. When all the students lined up to go, my teacher called my name and told me to line up with the students going on the field trip! This was the beginning of my faith journey! I said this to connect you with how God has caused me to believe him no matter what!! Don't look at the circumstances. It doesn't matter how small or large or disastrous it may be God hears and delivers!

I was too young to understand faith and that this would be the beginning of my journey of faith with God. This was the beginning of many faith events. I've said this to connect you with other trials that made me believe God no matter what the situation.

In May of 1992 a few days after the Rodney king riot in Los Angeles I had just delivered my fourth child. Exactly ten days later I woke up in a puddle of blood, it was so intense that I literally thought I was peeing on myself. I could remember getting up and walking over to the phone in the hallway while the blood was running down my legs like water flowing out of a faucet. When I reached the phone I dialed 911 The operator told me to lie on the floor and extend my legs upward to slow down the bleeding., Somehow after calling the paramedics, I managed to call my mother to let her know what was going on. Now in the mist of all of this I remained calm I asked my mother to take care of my children because I had no clue of what was going to happen. But oddly death had not entered my mind. After making the phone calls I continued with the instructions of the 911 call. While I was on the floor, I prayed, I asked God to allow me to stay here to raise my children. Finally the paramedics came and the next thing that I could remember was waking up in the intensive care unit. My mother was standing there; her exact words were she didn't think that I was going to live. My skin was gray and my eyes were dull but I was so glad to be in the land of the living. To see the sun shining out of the window and I could breath fresh air nothing else mattered. God had answered my prayer! I'm still here. After being in intensive care for nearly two weeks I was sent home with a catheter bag on my side. I didn't care; I was alive!

Barely being able to move around while at home, I witnessed the hand of God on a daily basis, I became stronger each day. My body was weak but my spirit grew stronger. I prayed, read the word and sang songs to the Lord! And he did a quick work! Not so much on my body but in my spirit I begin to know him on different levels! His word became more real to me than ever. I had nothing else to do, but to trust him! I believe that sometimes God allows things to happen so that we could know him for ourselves. I could remember my great grandmother saying" He's a doctor in the sick room" and I would pray using those words not knowing him on that level. But now I know He really is a healer!

I remember crying and in pain trying to use the restroom with the catheter. I begin to pray for the removal of the bag. God reminded me of the scripture" this sickness is not until death but for the glory of God" (St John 11:4) I begin to rejoice! Immediately, I felt happy and joyful!

When I look over the years of my life, I could remember so many times when God stepped in and moved miraculously! It's crazy to believe that he used something as small as a field trip to activate my faith. Now I know him on a personal level, I can share with others the works of my father. I know that his word is true if we believe!

MEMOIR II

ANGELA'S MEMOIR
THE BIRTH

Sing oh barren, you who have not borne. Break forth into singing and cry aloud You who have not labored with child. "For more are the children of the desolate, than the children of the married woman," says the Lord

Isaiah 54:1 KJV

THE WOMB CONNECTION

4 lbs. 13 oz. bag of goodies

carmel skin almond shaped eyes

red gumdrop cheeks…

nestled with delight inside my womb

less than a 5 lb. bag of brown sugar

equal in taste greater in content….

Life is just too precious to be forgotten, especially when it's blooming inside your womb. I penned this poem nearly thirty years ago for my daughter and kept a journal prior to my children's births. My first child, Adia was born December 29. She and my two sons (Alijah and Aharon) have brought bountiful blessings into my life. I still don't fully grasp the depth of Jesus' love but being a mother has brought me into the realm of understanding. The ***womb connection*** transformed my life.

Each pregnancy was special because we were so intricately connected. I never had any problems until it was time to deliver. I'm still boggled by the fact that I had three children yet I never experienced labor which is the most anticipated event of pregnancy. The body usually provides several clues that the onset of labor is approaching, but my body never received the signals! The doctors tried to induce labor, still I did not respond to the triggers. What happens when there is no labor? The pain is often unbearable but muscles need to contract to help PUSH the baby down the canal. Without labor the baby gets stuck and cannot move forward. The child's life is in danger--as was my daughter's.

Adia was only a few seconds away from death. The day she was born I had an appointment for a two-week overdue checkup. Mind you, I was nine months, plus! I was so ready to drop the load and it wouldn't come out! The doctor on duty and the medical team constantly checked me because the only sign that I was ready to give birth was that the mucous plug dislodged. For several hours they tracked my progress by an external monitor, but I only dilated one centimeter. To acquire an accurate reading they decided to use an internal monitor.

They immediately detected that my daughter's heart rate had dropped to zero! Immediately the doctor called for an emergency Cesarean section. Adia was in "distress" and I couldn't bear the thought of her dying in my womb. I wept.

As mothers we constantly pray and weep for our children. We feel their pain and agony and want it to cease. Mother's wit lets us know when they are in trouble. It's that *"womb connection."* We desire to shield them from the woes of the world, like a mother bird covers her young but we have to allow them to spread their wings, fly and leave the hallowed nest- although they may fall.

During labor attention is given to the mother, but have you ever wondered what the child feels and experiences traveling through a very narrow canal that's almost impossible to tunnel through! The Lord said that a woman would labor in birth but I believe the baby endures it own struggles. I've never heard of a child that came out the womb cooing or laughing. It cries! When she was lifted out of my womb, it was obvious that life was being sucked out of Adia's body. Her skin was withered and my placenta had begun to deteriorate. Death was beginning to make its abode. But God said no, *"I shall live and not die"*

Tears are welling up in my eyes right now because my mind journeys back to when I almost lost my daughter--again. Not to death, but to life. At the age of sixteen the woes of life took a toll, and the pressure of being in a unique position carried more weight than I imagined. She was the first born, only daughter and a PK. Who really knows what its like to be a PK? (Preachers Kid). A divine call is placed upon the father and mother so what is the enemy's strategy? To simply destroy the seed. These children have an anointing upon their lives so he makes every attempt to either assassinate, abort, or cause a miscarriage. If the scheme isn't successful, Satan tries to lame, cripple or hinder what God ordained.

During her last year of high school I dreamed that my daughter was living in a ditch, covered with sewage and the vicissitudes of life. In reality the enemy was trying to drain the very life out of her. But knowing that she was ordained, (Adia means "A Gift from God") my husband and I fought for her physical, emotional and spiritual health. After many years, of intercessory prayer, fasting and speaking The Word into her life she was delivered and saved! The prayers of the righteous availed much; I praise God other spiritual midwives helped to bear the burden.

Mothers don't be ignorant of Satan's devices, you must be maintain that *womb connection.* Stay spiritually sensitive and constantly protect your children (from conception until adult years) because Satan has a contract out to kill them. Hold on to the promise for your children and your children's children as many as the Lord our God shall call. (Joel

As a first lady and spiritual mother I constantly intercede for children to be birth into the Kingdom of God. At times the labor is unbearable and when it looks like nothing is happening or the babe is stuck in the birth canal it consoles me to know that my labor is not in vain. Yes, it's hard, but it's a labor of love.

So women keep the ***womb connection*** and labor for your child's spiritual health.

PUSH --**P***ray* **U***ntil* **S***ouls* **H***eal.* Stay connected and give birth to your hopes and dreams. The pain may be intense but you will rejoice when it comes forth!

MEMOIR III

SASHA'S MEMOIR
A SINGLE MOHER'S LIFE NEVER ALONE

"Being confident of this very thing, that he which hath begun a good work in you will perform it until the day of Jesus Christ."

Philippians 1:6 KJV

First thought that came to mind when asked to be in this project. “Mmmmm, I have had a very experienced life with many ups and downs “. Now what part should I write about. So after thinking for a few days I decided to start at the age of 26.

While standing here in the mirror combing my hair and admiring myself, not really caring too much about what I see in the mirror. To others, I may be attractive but to me I look too big; I really need to lose some weight. Oh well girl, you better make the best of what you got and look good for your girl’s big 30 parties at the most popping-est place in town. Finally, after two and a half hours of changing clothes over ten times and my room looking a hot mess, I said, “I’m READY, Let’s go”. As we all finally meet up together and make it inside, we are having the time of our lives without a care in the world; I mean not one. Last call for alcohol was stated over the microphone. “ Dang that means it’s almost time for us to go in for the night”. Oh well another lonely night for me again, since I found out that the fool I have been dealing with has a wife and way too many children for anybody to keep up with at all.

Anyway enough of that stage, while walking to the parking garage a big black hummer pulls up on the side of us while we are walking, This dude leans out his passenger side window and he say “ Hey momma, what’s going on? Come holla at me for a minute”. Me being as silly and as shy as I am, looked around and said; “Who you talking to me?” He said, yeah you come here. So I go to talk to him and we talk for a good five minutes. We exchanged numbers and we went on our way. Thirty minutes later he calls my phone and asks me where I am headed, I say home. He says, “Where is home?” I said, “Where my house stays.” He laughs and says, “No, I mean do you stay in Oakland or what?” I said, ”Oh my bad. I stay in Oakland. He says, “Alright ma, I will be calling you tomorrow.” I smiled and said. Ok.”

The next day came which was Sunday, I went to church and then drove all the way to Stockton to hang out with him all day. From then on, we were together all the time. We had many conversations about my life. But come to think about it, we never had any conversations about his life except one painful event that was hard for him to deal. With that said, we ended up talking about family and children and things like that. He really wanted a little girl and since I was his girlfriend I was determined to give him that. By the time April came and we had many ups, downs and family tragedies. I found out that I was pregnant.

I was 26 years old and pregnant. I remember this part of my life as if it was yesterday. The day I found out that I was having a baby I was perfectly fine. The next day I was sick as a dog and other things. No food would stay down, no fluids would stay down. I was depressed because I had to work every day. Getting up in the morning was a struggle. Every morning I would get up to go to the bathroom and sit on the floor for at least 45 minutes throwing up and crying. I strongly disliked throwing up. Then to the closet and back to the floor I went for another 45 minutes to think of what to wear, 'cause nothing fit. Two hours of that for 8 ½ months, and being late every day and having to get fluids through an IV twice a week. The doctor finally decided that I was way too sick to continue on carrying this little angel; because the baby wasn't growing as expected.

On December 23, 2007 I was to be induced. And on December 24, 2007 AEB was born and she was the lightest baby that I had ever seen. The doctor asked if I would like to hold her and I stated, "Not till you clean her off". He did and I held her. She was so precious and I was excited.

Two days later, I was released from the hospital. After being home for about two weeks I realize that my little princess was only drinking one ounce of milk every ten minutes and has not had a bowel movement since we left, and when she finally did it came out in a clay color sac, I took her to the doctor and after different opinions I found out that my baby had a disease called "Biliary Artesia"(**Biliary atresia, also known as "extrahepatic ductopenia" and "progressive obliterative cholangiopathy" is a congenital or acquired disease of the liver and one of the principle forms of chronic rejection of a transplanted liver allograft, it has an occurrence of 1/10,000 to 1/15,000 cases in live births in the United States. In the congenital form, the common bile duct**

between the liver and the small intestine is blocked or absent. The acquired type most often occurs in the setting of autoimmune disease, and is one of the principle forms of chronic rejection of a transplanted liver allograft... From Wikipedia, the free encyclopedia).

She had to undergo a surgery called the Kasai Procedure (**a surgical treatment performed on infants with biliary atresia to allow for bile drainage. In these infants, the bile is not able to drain normally from the small bile ducts within the liver into the larger bile ducts that connect to the gall bladder and small intestine. From Wikipedia, the free encyclopedia**). For three months straight, I was at the hospital with her for 14 hours a day, 7 days a week. I was tired, and drained. Due to all the things that were going on with her, I had to take a voluntarily leave from my job because I had no more maternity leave, child bonding leave or family leave. Which I believe was a good move at the time. I remember thinking "Wow, out of all the people and children in the world, my child had to be the one out of the ten thousand that just had to get this disease. Why God?, I have always been a good child and person, I have never disrespected my family or did anything wrong. I always gave my last and even when I was tired, I still did what was asked of me. Oh well I hope you have a better plan for what is going on." At the end of March 2008 I was finally able to take my baby girl home with instructions to give her about seven; yes I said seven medications twice a day. We had two doctor appointments a week. But she was better and a lot happier. All through this time, things were going just fine. Then all of a sudden she had a temp of 102 and nothing was breaking this fever down at all. So to the emergency room we went. And again I found out that she had Cholangitis (**inflammation of the bile duct**). So for ten days we sat in the hospital so that they could give her antibiotics through IV. She has had this bacterial infection 4 times so far in her life and the doctors say that will not go away (I believe God is a healer and a way maker.)

In June of 2011, my mother and I went to a very important doctor's appointment for AEB. See the doctors told me in one of our many appointments that at the age of 1 she would need a liver transplant. Her I year birthday came and went and they gave me another at the age of 3. Now at this appointment, we meet with the liver team specialist of Stanford hospital who conducts liver transplants and places children and adults on the donors list. After speaking with them they stated that she was very healthy and they did not see her ever having to get a transplant. Oh my heart was so relieved and my soul was thanking God for seeing fit to let MY MIRACLE PRINCESS LIVE. I have never really shared this story of my life because the timing was never right. But when this project came alone I felt that this would be the perfect opportunity to share my story with the world.

A Woman of Strength

By: Lady Elder Bessie Sims

A Phenomenal Woman

You are a Woman of strength who has the ability to stand strong, with your head up high knowing you have the power to resist the attacks of hopelessness, low self-esteem, and the feelings of being overwhelmed and that no one seems to care. So look at yourself in the mirror and say, Oh yes, I am a woman of strength; I fight off all the attacks by going down on my knees; I have the courage to face the day and the confidence to handle whatever comes my way; Life holds to boundaries and God don't make mistakes so now today I say the way I am is the way He made me and I am changing & evolving everyday into what He called me to be ; so I will pronounce myself the way He sees me; I am a woman strength shining with power, faith, hope and endurance, oh yes I have overcome, my mind is at peace, I am blessed and highly favored, I am a trailblazer, I am a warrior, worshipper, praiser and everything He calls me to be and whatsoever I put my hands to do shall be blessed!! Oh yes, that's me pure and holy presenting myself to thee, a virtuous woman calling it to be; therefore, I declare that is me, a Woman of Strength who knows that while on this journey I will face some battles, hurt, setbacks, and disappointments but it is in the journey where I find me and I am made strong as He has chosen me to be!!
A Woman of Strength – Phenomenally!!

MEMOIR IV

ANGELA'S MEMOIR
BOUND BUT NOT BROKEN:
GOD'S PURPOSE FOR MY LIFE

If you say, "The LORD is my refuge,"

and you make the Most High your dwelling, no harm will overtake you, no disaster will come near your tent. For he will command his angels concerning you to guard you in all your ways;

Psalm 91:9-11 NIV

The importance of knowing who you are and whose you are.

Health in relation to spiritual warfare

I was told my whole journey into this world was that of a best seller. My mom was four months before she knew of me and then had me at eight months. My father was abusive, so my mom had decided after her fifth miscarriage that she was done having kids. She had an IUD when I was conceived. Needless to say, I was supposed to be here. I was told that when I came out I had the IUD on my ring finger as if I was married to the idea that anything was possible. As if that wasn't enough, I was only 13inch long and was told that I would not grow, and to top it off my lungs were not developed. Are you starting to get the picture? From the beginning I was defying all odds. God had started a work that I know, only He, could get me through. Much like the beginning, I have had a long list of illnesses. I had pneumonia as a baby, and all of the childhood diseases in the world. In high school I had a stroke; college I had a miscarriage which lead to the discovery of cancer; early adulthood I have had kidney surgery, 2 C-sections removal of right side (fallopian tube and ovary) diabetes, high blood pressure, high cholesterol, and the latest, brain tumor/migraine and (at the time of me writing this) I'm being tested for Lupus. Are you kidding me! Not to mention all of the unknown illness that was unable to be explained along the way. And look at me, I bear no scars. It is God who has carried me through. The word of God says Jesus took my infirmities and bore my sicknesses. Therefore I refuse to allow sickness to dominate my body. The life of God flows within me and brings healing to every fiber of my being. Matt 17; John 6:63 Growths and tumors have no right to my body. They are a thing of the past for I am delivered from the authority of darkness. Col 1:13, 14 No evil will befall me; neither shall any plague come near my dwelling. For you have given Your angels charge over me. They keep me in all my ways. In my pathway are life, healing and health. Psalms 91:10, 11, Proverbs 12:28

What is Healing? What does it mean to be healed? What does it feel like to be healed? And more importantly how do you maintain/fight to keep the healing? Well, Webster's saying healing is to make or become well or healthy again; to cure (An disease) or mend, as a wound.

From the time I can remember I remember the feeling that there was someone watching over me. I can't explain it, but I just knew. I remember being able to look at people and just know things about them. I couldn't explain why or how I knew what I knew, I just knew. Sometimes it would be good and then there were times it wasn't good. The good thing was I wasn't alone. My sister also had this gift. But she would have dreams. Our house hold was full of the abnormal (which I now know as warfare). At a young age I was subjected to a lot. It was so bad, at times, that I really don't remember a lot of my childhood. In the Psychology world this is often know as post-traumatic stress disorder. I call it favor. I believe that there are times when the Lord will take things that don't belong to us away. In Ps. 68:11 it says blessed be the Lord, who daily bears our burdens, even the God who is our salvation. Selah: (which means to pause and think about what was just said) look at the God we serve, I truly believe this is what happened. The Lord was like you are too young to deal with such foolishness; and just like that He took them. Poof gone, the memories of violence and abuse toward my mother and brother are no longer there to haunt me (as they do my siblings). Why me Lord? Why don't I remember the stories I've been told? To this day I don't really have an answer, but I'm sure glad I don't. I often think, "What would have become of me if I carried all of the pains and mental bruises my mother carries?" For her they are worn as a tightly fitted coat, able to be put on at will. But the demons they pose aren't as easy removed. One can't imagine the way she feels when she sees my Father. Although he has changed, I know it's not the same view or image I see. When I look at him, I see a father who has been through a lot and carries a lot of missed opportunities. I see a man who has been given the favor of God in many ways but haven't yet accepted the Father who has given them. I see a man that if given a chance; and could allow himself to look past today and what it doesn't hold and look to what God says about his life and his future; could be a powerful man in Christ. But, what does she see? And better yet, when she looks at herself, who is the woman in the mirror?

Well before I tell you what I see in my Mom I will answer the burning question I know you're probably asking yourself. Why am I I talking about this? After all this is supposed to be a chapter about me. Well that's just it. I have learned that I am a product of my Mother and Father. And even though I have also learned that My Heavenly Father is the real master mind behind my gifts and character. We shouldn't be fooled into thinking that the men and women whom raised us don't have a part to play in the people we've become. Before we knew about the characteristics of Our Father, The heavenly attributes that we possess and hopefully model now; we often model those traits of our earthly parents.

Yes...I know we would all like to think that we came out being humble, loving, giving, and exhibiting holiness. This would be wonderful, and in many cases true until we learned and began to walk in (what I like to call) the atmospheric attributes. The attributes of selfishness, loneliness, fear, jealousy, and pride and the all-time favorite, abandonment and these are just to name a few. Well, one would ask...where did these attributes come from? I know when I first started to display fear...I often asked myself, what I'm so afraid of. Or when I would hear a man yelling at a woman the reaction of anger can up so quick that your head would spin I would think, why do I feel like this? The attribute or spirit of Lust...ya this was a big one. And in fact this one followed me until a year ago. Ya lust was big, but how did I get a hold to that attribute? Where did it come from? After all I was a good kid. I never cut school; I got almost straight A's. I was voted most spirited, best vocalist and prettiest eyes in High school. No, get this I wore a whinstone Jesus button everyday on all of my shirts. I mean every day!! Now ask yourself, How could a good girl who was a virgin until she was 20year old

(Which was amazing even in my day) struggle with the spirit of lust? Well in order to explain that, I need for you to know exactly what the word attributes is. The word attributes means to consider as a quality, or characteristic of a person, thing group, etc or to regard as resulting from a specified cause. So when you look at the def and then think back on the characteristics we display, we can easily come to the conclusion that many of our traits displayed to one another comes from a person and or an specified cause or event. Wow...you got that right.

I found out that while I was yet a little girl, things that I didn't have any control over were managing to control me. Fear, anger, abandonment, lust, confusion, low self-esteem were rapidly becoming friends, or let's say creating a bond that I would find out later only God could break.

Where do I start? My story would truly take more than a chapter if I was to break it down, so I'll give you the highlights. Now in the beginning I told you that me being here was an act of God in itself. By the time I was six, I had been fondled. Now even though there was no penetration, the spirit of Lust had got its foot in the door. Because I had so much fear and low self-esteem that spirit wasn't allowed to come out (then!!) but it would lie dormant until another time. Fear was alive and kicking. I told you before that I didn't remember all of the things that happened in my household, and I still don't. Thank God! But what I do remember is more than enough. I remember seeing things that I know shouldn't have been there. I would hear the grown-ups talk about seeing ghosts. I remember thinking is that what it is? I remember always being afraid to go to sleep last, so I would make sure I went to sleep before everyone. This would assure that someone in the house was up to watch over me. I was very sensitive to people and things even at that age. Remember when I told you that I wasn't alone. Well now I realize I wasn't. My sister had seen the same things. She has always been very vocal, so she would tell my mom. "Mom I seen this figure by my bed, it wasn't nice. But my mom would act like she didn't hear my sister or that my sister was making it up. This went on until the day my sister woke up looking like a monster. I know it sounds crazy, but it true. The crazy part is when our grandma got on the phone to pray for her, she couldn't stand to hear it, she threw down the phone. When we got her to the hospital, the doctors couldn't explain what was going on. Know one could. To this day we still don't know what happened. All we know, (my Mom sister and I) is the house wasn't ok! And it appeared the women in the house were taken a beating, in the physical and the natural. It wasn't long before my Mom and Dad split up. The only way my mom came back was that my dad promised her we would move. I remember the week we were moving, the neighbor came out and asked my mom were she and our Father still together? My mom didn't think this was strange, because her house was a place of refuge many nights. My mom, almost embarrassed, replied yes. The neighbors look at my mom and said...You guys are the only ones. No other couple has ever stayed together after living there. It wasn't until I got grown that I heard that while living in that house, my mother wasn't just getting attacked by my father, she was seeing and dealing with the same unexplainable things, but in a greater way. Attributes of **fear** and torment check.

Even after the move, the abuse didn't completely stop. Finally my mom got tired and decided to leave and move to Washington. At the time I thought that we were just going to visit her friend and help her out for a while; that's what I was told. I didn't know that my mom was leaving my dad. Not that it would have made me much difference, for I feared my father back then. It was the separation from my family that got to me. It seemed that once we were gone, it was out of sight, out of mind. I felt like we no longer mattered. Little did I know, that my mother felt that was her whole life. Attribute of **abandonment**, check.

So what next? We are a long way from home and it's just my mom and I. The living situation and helping my mom's friend is not what it looks like. Why are my mom and I getting our own place? I thought we were here to help your friend? Why can't I call home and talk to my dad? Why are you changing the number? What is the big deal? I have to go to school? This was supposed to be a quick thing. Why does it feel like we are moving here? Are my sister and brother coming? What about Dad, I mean he's mean and all but what about him? Did you just leave your other kids? You said that we would only be down here until our house got finished and we would be helping your friend just until then. Mom...what is going on? I never got a clear answer. The attribute of confusion was alive and kicking. Maybe what I feel doesn't matter. After all I'm just seven and who cares that I miss all my family? Who cares that I miss my friends? Who cares that all I see is my mom looking sad? See, it's just like I said. Out of sight, out of mind. No one cares about us, and she doesn't even care about me. By the way...who is that guy that keeps coming by? I don't think I like him.

We had been in Washington for several years; by this time I had given up on the idea of us going back to Cali. My mom had started dating and it was obvious that she and my father weren't together anymore. Several people had come to court my mom, each worse then the first, in my opinion. I had figured out that I was good at picking them. And I didn't like any at this point.

Then, my sister lived with us. At first it was great, but then something changed. Both my mom and sister were no longer the same people I remembered. It was as if they had gone on vacation and came back totally different people. They began arguing all the time and things were becoming out of hand. My old friend fear had come back into the house, this time he brought some friends; Drugs and alcohol. Now don't get me wrong, I had been around drinking before. My mom's parents were avid drinkers. But this was different. When my grandparents drank they were funny. It was like watching Laurel and Hardy. With my mom, it was different. My mom wasn't funny, she was angry and belligerent. She would get drunk and yell all the time. The yelling became so bad that my sister began yelling as well. It became a yelling match. One thing good did come out of this; in my desperation to prevent my mom from drinking I would steal her liquor and cook with it. I was too afraid to throw it out, so this was the beginning of my famous Brandy Fried Chicken; Look at God. To add more fuel to the fire my sister was seeing this older man who I soon found out was trouble, with a capital T. Not only did he introduce my sister to drugs, he worshiped the devil. Yes! Satan had entered our home and was dead set on tearing us apart. My mom began hitting me when drunk (and not remembering the next day), which lead to the first time my sister hit my mom (protecting me); my sister's boyfriend tried to kill my sister and mom when she tried to break-up with him (by trying to run them off a snow/icy road). My mom's new boyfriend seemed to be the only light in this sea of darkness, but he just wasn't enough. Fear, confusion, abandonment, drugs, anger and alcohol had taken our home under siege and the only way out for me was to move back to California. Yes, strength had come on the scene. At the time I didn't know where it came from, I just knew I needed it.

The move back to California was hard. After moving from place to place/house to house; feeling unloved and unwanted for a year and a half I finally got settled at my dad's moms (grandma's). DO it Jesus! I can finally rest. Well this was true for a min. Wait, it's not like I didn't rest, I did. All I had to do was go to school and church. Piece of cake. Life was great. I was enrolled in Upward bound where I began to travel to different states. Yes finally I was seen for me. Finally someone cared enough about me to put me first. I began to learn about the Lord; the dreams hadn't come yet, so I really had no cares. Well at least none at my grandma's. It wasn't until I visited other family members' homes that I felt like I didn't fit in. I felt like I was different. Don't get me wrong, no one ever said that but I just felt it. I felt like I wasn't small enough or pretty enough, or dressed good enough. Once again low self-esteem, was renting a room in my head, and I began to feel alone. I would find myself coming to family functions on my mom's side that I didn't know about. Leaving feeling left out and not wanted. That old feeling of abandonment was back. But this time I had a new fight. This time I would fight back. Instead, of feeling sorry for myself, I would plunge myself into school. I would be all that I could be. And so I did. By the time I graduated from high school, I had managed to achieve not only the Principal's Award, but I had gone to Washington D.C for an essay contest, and was interviewed by channel 2 for up and coming student in Oakland. Yes this was great; I was on my way to college and feeling great. Nothing could stop this feeling of bliss.

Well that was until I suddenly had a stroke. Yes, a stroke. How could this happen, what the crap was going on? You see in all of this working hard, I had discovered how to push down all of my feelings. The stress of being away from my mom and dad, pushed down. The stress of my older brother living a life on the streets, pushed down. The stress of my sister and mother fighting and having to move what seemed like every month, pushed down. The stress of taking the S.A.T's and passing and having enough money to really go to college, pushed down. You see on the outside I had mastered looking good and feeling good, but on the inside I had managed to push down all of the feelings that I didn't want to deal with. See what I didn't say was when I left my Mom although it took strength; it also gave me a tool I would use until it crashed. It taught me to run from my issues. If I didn't like something, I just walked away from it. Problem solved. I didn't know that the problem didn't really go away; it just was shifted to a different channel. So as I laid on the gurney, and the doc was talking to my grandma about the stroke, I had my first talk with God. I mean real talk. I told Him if he got me out of this, I would spend more time talking and trying to get to know Him like my grandma. You see, my grandma talked to Him every day. She wouldn't put her foot on the floor until she asked God what to do. I use to tell her , "Grandma you bother God so much , He don't have time to talk with anyone else." Boy, what was I getting myself into? From that first talk, it seemed like I had new eyes.

When I told you that I use to see things on people, well, it continued. But now I would get thoughts in my head to go along with those feelings. I often told my grandma about the things I had seen and thought. I remember she would just look at me and shake her head. I would think what? Little did I know that my whole stay at her house was a set-up. I was in training for my future. All of the near death encounters were just attacks. Yes, you heard me; I told you that I would just give the highlights. But believe me, there were more then a few times that I know my grandma was praying for me. One time I was at home, trying to figure out a way to ask my grandma to go to the school dance. You would think this was easy, but not for my house. The rule at my house was that I had to beat the street light on; yes...this was the whole time I lived there. So senior year was no different, and the fact that it was the homecoming dance didn't make a difference, either. So I was thinking of how to ask when I heard my grandma calling my name. I tried to ignore it but I kept hearing her. Long story short, I finally went back to see what she wanted, when I got back there I just knew she was going to bust me out for trying to plot and go to the dance. After all grandma knew everything. No not this time, she had other things on her mind; like saving my life. Once in the back she told me to sit down and not move. I sat there for which seemed like a lifetime. After about an hour, she began to tell me that she only called me once, (so who kept calling me) and that she called me because someone was about to come and steal the motor bike that she told my brother not to bring into the gate. You see we had a six foot gate that wrapped around our house. And earlier that day she had told my brother not to bring this bike on her property. Needless to say, he didn't listen. Well as she sat there praying, God had showed her the bike being stolen, and me and our German shepherd are being shot. You can imagine the way I felt when right after she told me, I heard the shot. I began to burst out in tears, thinking that the dog had been shot. My grandma said "No that was the lock". She had locked Delta on the back porch when she first called me. My window was in the front of the house, and in her vision when I heard the first shot (the one we just heard) I went to the window and looked out. The next shot was going to be me and the third the dog, which had lunged at the man. As I fell to the bed crying, I thank the Lord, for allowing me to hear His voice, for I knew it had to be Him that kept calling me over the loud radio. To God be the glory. That was just one of the many times God had allowed my grandma to stand in the gap for me. I tell you when God has a plan for your life, it will be completed.

In college I was like wow, I'm free. Although I love my grandma and for the most part I loved the shelter effect; I was 19 yrs old and it was time I acted like it. After all I was a good girl. How much trouble could I get in? Ha...it didn't take long for me to be reintroduced to lust and low self-esteem. A powerful combination. Now how can you have lust and low self-esteem at the same time? Easy...I still didn't think that I measured up to the other girls. I mean now I was on a college campus, and all the popularity of being in high school was gone. And even worse, I still needed to feel popular, and to feel like I was on top and beloved. Being in a new place and knowing only a handful of people made me feel small and insurmountable. But It wouldn't take long for me to meet people and create a whole new person. Yes, it wasn't enough that I would begin to drink, smoke weed, steal and have sex. I created a whole personality to encompass this new me. I became Sparkle. And Sparkle was everything Angela wasn't. Sparkle was confident, outgoing, sexy, and willing to try anything, once. Sparkle was something else. Sparkle was also sick in more ways than one.

Not long after becoming Sparkle, which by the way was a nick name originated from my mother and her love for the movie; it was also the name giving to me in high school for my bubbly personality. But it in college it didn't carry the same meaning.

I was in my second year; I hooked up with this young man who was a key player on the football team. Wow, he liked me, and he was really cute. Don't get me wrong, when I left for school I was engaged and had a promise ring from my high school sweet heart. You see I had been with this person since the end of tenth grade, but we never did ANYTHING. He treated me like a queen; he never tried to push me into anything. On my graduation night from high school, I called myself going to go all the way, I got part of the way and couldn't take it. He stopped and told me, we would be together forever so there wasn't any rush. So you can imagine the hurt I felt when I got to college and found out he was having a baby. I realized that he never pushed me, because he was still doing his ex. Although I felt he really loved me. He even explained that he couldn't take the non-physical aspect of our relationship; he still wanted to marry me. He was just waiting till I was ready...right. Well the baby's mama wasn't going for that. So after her playing games with his newborn, I decided that I wasn't going to be the reason for the baby mama drama. We parted ways; and this was the beginning of no more drama in my life. So, having a cute boyfriend wasn't new. This experience was something else. What was this new feeling? For the first time I felt like I was in control of me. I wasn't going to let anyone push me around, I wasn't going to let anyone hurt me again without letting them know where to go and how to get there. Oh...I like this. I can go and come as I please, and if I didn't want you around then kick rocks. Well although I was wearing this new role well, nothing would prepare me for my first full fledge spiritual attack. In what seemed like a mega second, I had had sex for the first time and found out I was pregnant. I had a miscarriage and found out I had cancer and was boyfriend-less all in one month. I mean for real? What the heck was I supposed to do with this? Not to mention the boyfriend who had gotten me pregnant, left at the first mention of cancer. I can't tell my family this! I had left for college as the golden child. I was considered so sweet, a good girl they don't know this Sparkle. Who would I tell this too? Well, of course, you know what I did. Right, I walked away from it. I got a doctor with my dad's insurance, went to my appointments and pushed all of the feelings down. After all I was told that I would be ok. Yes, I can do this. I won't tell a sole. Oh, well beside my best friend that heard the message of the results of my D & C (Dilation & Curettage) over our answering machine. Oh yes... Didn't I tell you? My (not so wonderful) doctor (whom I later fired) told me I had cancer on my answering machine. Imagine getting a massage that said...Hi Angela, this is Doctor (so and so) and I'm calling to inform you that as we did your D and C, we found cancer. We need you to come in right away. Here is my number. Hope to see you today. Wow... Are you for real? So... three weeks into this nightmare I am going to the cancer specialist, and I get this pain. It's at this time that I found out that the radiation I was getting had went into a cist, which now had become toxic. So now I went from being alone, to having my whole family find out in a matter of hours. My roommate got punked by my sister, who had being feeling like something was wrong with me. She had been calling me for weeks but I wouldn't answer. So the next thing I knew, I was being rushed into surgery and remained in the hospital for the next month. The strange thing was I remember thinking Ha...devil, you lost again. You came for my life and God saved it. Do it Jesus! It wouldn't be long for before the devil tried again.

During the month of me going through radiation, I was introduced to weed. I was told that cancer patients could get a cannabis card and everything. Needless to say it wasn't the medical marijuana I was smoking. My weed habit went up to a twenty sack a day. Accompanied with Jack Daniel mixed with Apple juice (which we named Applejacks) and pain pills. Yes, I was all messed up. But the crazy part was I was still going to school and was what you would coin a "functioning addict". No one knew what was going on. No one but the people I was getting high with and The Lord. But thank God that when he starts a work, he finishes it. After being laced, and almost dying, and getting alcohol poisoning and almost dying, I finally decided that I wasn't made of this scene. I wanted to live and not die. I asked God once again to come in. After many battles I went back and forth with the demons of lust, drugs, low self-esteem, abandonment and torment till finally I gave my life fully to Christ.

Now don't get me wrong. I would be lying if I told you that all was gravy then. Ha...no that is when the real battled started. I begin to be attacked in my sleep and the Lord had to really show me who I was fighting and more then that, He showed me who was fighting on my behalf. Yes, this is the real battlefield. But the great thing is I know who wins. You see through it all I have found out that I have a calling on my life. Haha...you think I would have figured that out a long time ago. See I hear that when your called you go through things. Why? Because the enemy knows who we are. The problem is, most of the time, we don't know. But then there is God. I thank God for His son Jesus who died so that I can be saved. I was able to be snatched out of the hand of the enemy who had me bound; and brought back into the light by the grace of Jesus. As a result, I have been blessed with a wonderful husband and two miracle children. See when I had cancer they told me I couldn't bear children, but once again God's mercy shined on me and I have been blessed with a girl and a boy. To God be the Glory.

So I asked before, what is healing? Healing is knowing the Doctor of all doctors. It being in Christ and allowing Him to mend all which was broken. How do you maintain it? You maintain healing by staying in the Word; Meditating on the Word day and night. The Lord gave us His Word as a guide, use it.

As for my Mother, what do I see when I look at her? I see a lot of myself. I see a strong woman who doesn't yet know her worth; A woman who was beaten, but not broken; A women who if she ever looked hard enough would see that she is more than enough in Christ Jesus; A woman who if willing to change from the victim would find that she is in fact the victor. In a lot of these ways we are alike; my mom and I. She is like the me I use to be before I found out who I was in Christ Jesus. I am a product of my parents. Yes, But now, I look like **Our Father.**

Now, as for Sparkle, she is gone. I only glimmer for Jesus!!! And although I still go through some stuff, I know where my help comes from. I see things in my dreams and in day that some people would run from. But thank God I no longer follow suit. I don't have to run anymore. In the Lord I have learned how to fight. I can now stand on the Word and know how to cast out spirits and call for my Lord and Savior who is my strong tower. I know now who I am. I'm an intercessor. I am a person who knows some of the wiles of the enemy; but will not allow him a foothold. I am an heir to the throne of Jesus. And in Christ, no weapons can prosper against me. Thanks be to God that I may have been bound, but I wasn't broken

MEMOIR V

BRENDA'S MEMOIR
MY LIFE

We often suffer, but we are never crushed. Even when we don't know what to do, we never give up. In times of trouble, God is with us, and when we are knocked down, we get up again. 2 Corinthians 4:8-9 CEV

When I was asked to write a chapter I was a little leery about telling a big chunk of my private life to God only knows how many people. I thought about it and my first thought was to just say no because my excuse was that I had members of my husband's family coming in for a Family Reunion and there would not be enough time for me to write about something so personal. I began to rationalize within the walls of my mind that there just is not enough time to write a whole chapter. Between going to work and trying to be social it would not allow me enough time to write anything, and that there would only be a few days left before the deadline. Which was only three days. And then on July 2 I, was hit with an epiphany.

For many years, I thought that I was learning how to be a dutiful wife by staying up late watching my mother get up out of her bed in the middle of the night to bake homemade biscuits, oatmeal, eggs, and chunks of bacon for my stepfather. He would come in high as a kite and wake my mother up just to fix him something to eat. Most of the time, he would fall asleep after only eating a few spoonful's of oatmeal and a bite here and there off the biscuits and ham. She would do it every time and never a harsh word spoken from her lips. I watched this take place for years. Little did I know, she was silently praying for a change. A change that would come at a price. Often times, I would feel sadden by the simple fact that she had to get up a few hours later and have to do it all over again; making sure all of her children were up and ready for school. I could only imagine the emotions that she kept bottled up inside. What I was learning, and here's the epiphany, was how to be still and quiet in the spirit!

In writing this chapter, I realized that the same Holy Spirit that guided my mother through her trials of life, had guided me through some of my darkest moments. For those of you reading this chapter that know me, know that I do not like being in the dark! I will turn every light on in the house during the day, even if the blinds are up. My darkness began like a slow motion movie, frame by frame. Then one day I realized that I was in the dark. Aw naw! This is not happening to me. It just can't be.

In 1982, I became involved with a star football player at my high school. It was against everything in me to allow myself to become involved. I did not like him in junior high but there's something about high school that makes you make idiotic decisions. I was a virgin. He masterfully took my virginity right from under my dress. Swoosh! And it was gone. No fireworks, nothing exciting. As a matter of fact, I did not like sex after the first go round because it hurt like the dickens. All he knew was to shove it in and bounce! Once he was done that was it. There was no conversation about how it felt or if I was satisfied. Just in and out. It was nasty. Then I became pregnant. How on earth was I going to tell my mom. She had enough to deal with dealing with my stepfather and his antics, my brother's defiance, and my oldest sister getting high as a kite and drunk as a skunk. Who was I to add to the problem? I needed to offer a solution. I ignored it and hoped and prayed that the pregnancy would go away. It didn't and I was getting bigger and bigger. Then there was the dreams about fish that my mother kept having. I felt sad, lonely, disgusted and like I had let everyone in my family down. I was hurting inside in the most terrible way. My life was stuck in a dark place and it seemed like the very one who had a major role next to me did not want to have anything to do with me now that he had gotten what he wanted sexually. He had urged me (along with his mother) to get an abortion. I just couldn't bring myself to do it. How could I just go to an abortion clinic and get rid of a part of my insides that God had given me. This boy began to hate me, and his family looked at me in disgust. How dare I make him, a good boy, suffer and not be able to go to college to pursue his football career. I felt like I had been placed in a machine that shrinks people, and then placed in a dark medicine bottle and tossed into the ocean. The most hurtful and disappointing thing was to come face to face with my mother, The woman who would silently work hard all day at work and then come home to run a big household. Way too many mouths to fill and here I was at sixteen adding another one to the bunch. When I made the decision to keep my baby, I lost friends and associates at school. I became depressed and did not want to tell anyone because I felt like I had done enough damage to my family. I had to just keep quiet. Church folks can be some of the most unforgiving people ever! Not only was I ostracized, but my mother and whole family were because a year prior to me getting pregnant, my oldest sister left Grambling State University because she was an unwed pregnant teen. Now here I was in the same boat, only younger. My family suffered a major internal blow during this time. My stepfather really began to act a fool. My oldest brother was getting out of control and my oldest sister was spiraling into an abyss of nothingness. Our family was struggling economically and socially, we were nondescript. We were just wafting through life as if someone had turned our speed down from sixty-five to five on the road of life.

In 1983, I gave birth to a beautiful baby girl, healthy and normal. I had dropped out of school for the most part of the eleventh grade in high school. A great number of rumors were going around that I was just another statistic and was not going to graduate. WHAT? No way was I going to do the eleventh grade all over again. Little did the naysayers know, I had all of the credits that I needed for eleventh and most of the twelfth grade years. I graduated on time with the rest of my class. The class of 1984!

The next frame began in 1986-1987. I was in downtown Oakland one afternoon coming out of a store when I met an older man who must have been in his sixties at the time. He stopped me and asked if I was looking for a job. Silly me, I said yes. He offered me a job being his secretary working out of his home. Yeah right! He said that he had a landscaping business and that I would be required to go out with him to various locations around the bay area. Little did I know, he had other motives. It did not take me long to discover that he was up to no good. This devil was slick, but God was on my side. He knew that I did not own a car at age twenty-one so he offered to buy me a used car. I remember going over to San Francisco looking at used cars with him and one of my aunts. He allowed me to pick out a car at a used car lot on Van Ness. I will never forget the car because had I gotten it, it would have been a classic by now and there would be a lot of offers to buy it from me. It was a forest green two-door Challenger. The interior had all the original parts and the black leather seats were in perfect condition. I really wanted that car and the price was only twenty-seven hundred dollars. He had previously told me that on any given day he would have over five thousand dollars in cash on him and that I would be required to make the deposits into his bank account. That was the main reason why he wanted me to have a car to get around in. I would also be required to run errands for him as well as take him to various job sites. Needless to say, I did not get the car because I would not sleep with him. He had asked me one day if I liked jewelry and I said yes. He asked if I liked diamonds and what color was my birthstone. The next thing I knew we were heading back over to San Francisco to the Jewelry Exchange to purchase a ring that had my birthstone in it. I went along with the idea because my aunt said that if he wants to spend his money on you let him. So I did.

There was something diabolical taking place here and the wheels of my mind began to unravel the mysteries within the scope of his intentions. This man was trying to marry me. He struck up a conversation with me one day about relationships between older men and younger women. I remember telling him that I did not think that there was anything wrong with it as long as the two parties involved loved each other wholly. With that said he took it upon himself to ask me if I could love him like that and marry him. The walls came tumbling down, down, down. No was my answer without any thought. Besides I had just started dating my youngest daughter's father. My aunt informed me later, that he so mad that he wanted to kill my daughter's father. How dare this man. How dare him to try to take my youth from me by slithering around like a king cobra waiting to strike! I looked back on some of the conversations that took place and none of them had anything to do with landscaping. He was always trying to get me to come over to his house alone and I never did. He asked me to come by to pick up some money that he wanted me to have so I asked my aunt to take me over there.

I remember having a gut feeling that something was not right. When I got there, he had a brown paper bag that had quite a bit of money in it. He asked me to come in and I told him that I would rather wait for my aunt to park the car first and then we would both come in. He became enraged and told me to get out and to take my aunt with me. I didn't know then what I had done to provoke his anger, but I certainly know now. I am so sure of it now that he wanted to get me alone to rape me. I won that battle by not becoming his victim.

The next frame came as my relationship with my daughter's father began to shift into parenthood. In 1988, I gave birth to a beautiful baby girl. This was it, so I thought. We were married shortly after she was born. Boy oh boy was I in for a major eye opener. This young man's mother was the apple of his eye and she could no wrong. Yeah, right! My emotions clouded my judgment. I should have paid more attention to what was unraveling before my eyes. He was every bit of his dad, a womanizer. I honestly believe that he tried very hard not to be that way, however, his hormones got in the way and in the end he gave in. I knew him more on an emotional level than the father of my other daughter. Financially, we would have been okay had he communicated more with me rather making financial decisions for us with his mom. He joined the Merchant Marines. He was set to make a phenomenal amount of money of which I would not have access. You see, he set up an account with his mother. He would deposit the money into his account and would tell me that if I needed any money I needed to go through his mother to get it. Go through his mother to get money to take care of our daughter? Really? There was something seriously wrong with this marriage. I felt as if I was living in the year of 1900. Why should I have to beg a hater for money to feed and clothe our child? I knew then that this would not be my life! There was no way I was going to go through this type of behavior for the rest of my life with this man. I think that we would have been better just as friends. I realized that it was time to make a drastic change. My marriage was going sour with my husband's philandering ways, his rude mother, and the automobile accident that had taken the lives of two of my sisters. Every part of my life was turning upside down and inside out. My survival mode kicked in and I had to make a decision that changed the very direction in which I was headed, to a psych ward! What did I do, I joined the Navy. After getting out of the glorious Navy, I had mixed feelings about the decision to join as well as my decision not to re-enlist. Needless to say, he divorced me and moved on.

The next piece of my life's map topped all others. I got back in the saddle so to speak. I met a man and fell in love and soon after we were married. MAJOR mistake! He was very abusive. The abuse that I endured was emotional, mental, and spiritual. You see, I married a minister. He was a gold digger as well. Way too many red flags flew past me. Before we got married, he would be missing in action for a week or two at a time and when I would ask him where he was, he would tell me that he just needed to get away. I was hurt and confused because he said that he loved me. Those were just cheerful words that he used to soothe me. As time went on, my emotions became raw and it felt like someone was pouring sea salt on them. At times when he was missing in action, I would page him and call him and he never would respond. I was devastated. I did not know if he had been in an accident, mugged or ill somewhere or what. I just needed reassurance that he was okay. I began to rationalize his disappearances, thinking that if we were married he would not do this to me. How naïve, I don't know what I was thinking because he would be at home doing absolutely nothing and would not pick me up from work or the subway station. Sometimes, I would sit stranded for hours waiting for a ride home from him. I prayed that he would take better care of me. That prayer was never answered.

Once we were married, he remained stable for a short period of time Life has a funny way of just happening. I would have never thought that a man of God would take me through such sorrow and pain. He was supposed to be my protector. I was supposed to feel safe with him. He belittled me in the confines of our home, never in public or around others. He would get up in church and say how much he loved his beautiful wife and that he loves me so much. At first I felt like he was making a change by starting right there in church. Man, was I wrong. He went back to his same old ways of disappearing. I became depressed and felt worthless. I had a constant battle within. One side of me was saying that my self worth was more valuable than anything that he could give or take away.

The other side would say that I should just stay in the marriage because I do not deserve anyone better than this. That battlefield that takes place in the mind is very dangerous.

I cried many lonely days and nights. I felt an implosion getting ready to take place. I became angry and bitter within. I housed a spirit that could have taken my life. He hated my girls and anything that made my heart smile. I felt so very alone. There was nothing anybody could do to make me feel better. I had to dig deep into my past to deal with the pain that I was enduring. I begged my husband to talk to me so that we could get our marriage back on track. There was no communication on his part except when he wanted my financial and emotional support for some entrepreneurial endeavor. And believe you me, he had many that required my financial support. In 2001, I got laid off my job and that meant that he had to help support the household. I was given a severance pay of eleven thousand dollars. Most of it was spent on him.

I should have followed my first mind and pay all the bills and rent for the months to follow until I became employed again. When I told him that I needed his help, he said that he would do more or better. This did not last because after the first month that he had to pay half all the bills, he was gone for a few days. When he returned, he had no excuse to give. I let it go at that because I needed to focus my energy on finding another job. One actually fell in my lap. I had not applied for this job; the manager from the previous office put a word out there that I was looking for a job. That was in 2002 and I am still with the same doctor. A lot less pay but God is good! A lot less pay meant that he would soon be out of there. At this point, there was no more intimacy in the marriage. I would literally have to beg to be touched. Eventually, I moved out of the bedroom and onto the couch. I cried deeply from my belly. When I reached way back in remembering what mama use to do, I did the same thing. I prayed hard. I prayed that God would remove me from this place of desolation. I prayed for God to take the pain away. I prayed for God to make the tears stop. I prayed for God to remove the cause and root of all that I was going through. In that moment, I knew that I had to get out of

God's way and be still. The prayers had been answered. One evening I came home with my oldest daughter from Bible study and he was gone. He had left with many household items and that was okay because I realized then that God heard my cry! The weight had been lifted. I could breathe another day.

I sent up a prayer to God with very specific requests about getting a husband. I wanted someone that had a genuine heart; a man with integrity, someone with which I could feel safe. He has to be able to walk on a tightrope, blindfolded and holding my heart in his hand. He has to have a level of love for me unmatched by any other. He needs to have compassion, wisdom and honesty. He has to be responsible, respectful and loyal to his word. He has to be patient. He has to be able to love me unconditionally. He would have to be able to protect me in every aspect of my life.

I was blessed to have my prayers answered once again. I met my current husband, Donald in the driveway of my sister's house. She had a speaking engagement in Vallejo, California, this particular Sunday afternoon. Donald had helped his Brother John hang a mirror in my sister's living room. They had come by to make sure that everything was okay because Donald had to move the thermostat on the wall a few inches. As they were coming up the driveway, John was talking to my sister and Donald extended his hand to me and introduced himself. In that very moment, I knew everything would be alright. I felt electricity that would make the fireworks that most people feel during their first kiss simply sizzle. It seemed as though God made the world stop just so we could see how awesome he really is. There was complete and utter silence outside. I'm talking no birds chirping, no bump-bump music, no noise from cars going by on the freeway, no noise from the train that usually goes by. We did not even hear the conversation that John and my sister were having. There was so much energy that surged through our hands that it had me thinking about this man all through church service. I sat in church thinking that I was going to go to hell for this.

I knew that he was the one immediately. I had gone through so much and had given so much of my essence to other people that I thought that I would not have enough left to give to Donald. God in his infinite wisdom has given me a new and refreshed level of love that goes beyond the borders of what I knew before. I almost lost Donald to a very real illness before we were even married. All I could think about was that God would not answer my prayers only to yank them back like some childish prank. It was no prank. Donald told me that he did not have any money and wanted to know if I still wanted to marry him in the state that he was in. I knew in my heart that he was the one and I told him absolutely. We were married twice in the same year in the middle of his illness. He had a pulmonary embolism, extreme weight loss, loss of muscle mass all over his body, unable to keep food down, unsteady on his feet, shakes and trembles, sometimes loss of thought process, a large mass removed from his neck, and surgery near his heart. He remained ill for a little over a year. God gave me grace and mercy. God gave me a man after his own heart. My husband reminds me of God's love and grace daily. He is strong. I am strong. Together, we are mighty!

A Woman Of Humility

By: Lady Elder Bessie Sims

A Phenomenal Woman

You walk humbly without fear & at times only with faith; You wrestle and battle but still you smile with elegance and grace; You restore hope, while healing hearts remaining us to believe; Though at times, it seems hopeless, but somehow you still succeed; You are resilient but proper, taking the lead; rejection, discrimination and envy – you made it through them all; Many often wonder how you bare such task and wear all those hats but somehow you fit them all; You wear different shoes to match every gift and of course you sprint in them all; Without giving it one thought you bravely stand ready to answer the call; to provide nourishment for the hungry & strength for the weak; You lead by example changing communities; making history just by living your dreams and rocking' them all; You are that Phenomenal Woman continue to walk tall! You are a Woman Phenomenally!!

MEMOIR VI

CACHET'S MEMOIR
TRANSFORMATION OF THE MASTER'S FEET

[For my determined purpose is] that I may know Him [that I may progressively become more deeply and intimately acquainted with Him, perceiving and recognizing and understanding the wonders of His Person more strongly and more clearly], and that I may in that same way come to know the power outflowing from His resurrection [[a]which it exerts over believers], and that I may so share His sufferings as to be continually transformed [in spirit into His likeness even] to His death, [in the hope] Philippians 3:10 AMP

Every woman wants and desires to feel special and unique. Grooming ourselves and emphatically creating our look according to the very idea and image of whom we want to look like. From the moment we see the first doll, to the day we design our picture perfect wedding. We are consumed with who we are and what we will one day become. Every little girl wants to be a princess and every young lady wants to be a bride. So often this guiding light is what our sights are focused on. We don't realize that every dream doesn't always become reality. Sometimes they become the nightmare we never envisioned. Life has a way of working out, not the way we planned, but according to the way God already designed it.

With every journey there is a predestined path set for us to follow, but because of our "Free Will" that God has given to each of us, we have choices. Those very choices create consequences that can altar and detour our direction on this journey. God tells us even in this, that He will make a way of escape that will reroute you to getting back on track with Him. We must be willing to allow every step to be orchestrated by Him, being sold out for him and walk in love. We must be forgiving and offer a repented heart. That gets you headed in the right direction. Distractions can cause you to change your direction or abort your own destiny. If you recognize the cunningness of the adversary, you can see him for what he is and respond accordingly. Life has a way of bringing opposition to make us feel defeated or in bondage to stop us from progressing or cause us to forsake a Christian lifestyle for temporal things.

Learning to remain committed to the cause for Christ's sake is our goal. For those who believe, He has given us power to trample the enemy and to live a life according to the scriptures which is in integrity and sincerity. God created us for His pleasure and for His purpose that we would serve Him with gladness and worship Him wholeheartedly. In Luke 10:38-42, Christ sent those that He appointed to go before Him to share of the kingdom of God and His coming. When Jesus arrived at Martha's house, she had a decision to make and she chose to continue preparing, while Mary made the choice to lie at His feet. Martha allowed herself to be distracted and yet Mary was focused on what she deemed more important which was being in His presence. This is how we, as Christians, are at times. We seek for God's attention, His affection and to dwell in that secret place with Him, but we get off track by making the wrong decisions and getting distracted by things that should've, could've been done or things that truly can wait. To reverence Him in worship is far greater than anything we could do. Mary recognized the significance and relevance of humbling herself before Him for what she believed to be more valuable and important to her. What a great example of the power of our choices and the reality of what being ready brings. Seizing the moment and taking advantage of every opportunity. God desires us to get to a place of readiness in Him so that when He shows up, we're not working towards His arrival, but already worshipping the mere presence of His arrival. The power, purpose and possibilities that come with being a phenomenal woman of God is knowing that you're confident in whom God has made you, focused on that which He has placed within you and available for everything He opens before you, not that you may boast in yourself, but the one who has made the impossible, possible for you.

Many things have occurred in my life that could have easily taken my attention, caused me to become defeated or to just lose hope of better days. One thing that I have to constantly remind myself is that "ALL THINGS are working together for my good". We may not see it now or while we go through, but in the end everything is made clearer by God. If we faint not, we will soar high like eagles.

At the age of 32, I found out that I'd started a process that would leave me totally blind. Within a few years it had increased at an exceptional rate. It left the doctors baffled and I found myself wondering had God brought me to this wilderness place of segregation that would leave me dependent on others and feeling forsaken. How could this be? If it wasn't enough to deal with this loss, after nearly 16 years of marriage I found out that my husband was secretly in an affair that would leave me unable to recognize the very mate that God sent me who had been living a double life. Thrust into a place of desperation, isolation and turmoil, I began to withdraw into myself. This could not very well be the love that God wanted husbands to show their wives. Feeling like I had just woke up from a dream to be thrown into a living nightmare and yet asking God, "Why me?" as He replied "Why not?" Broken down to the point where I felt pushed into a corner with nowhere to go, no one to talk to and no sense of how I would move forward. This wasn't what I had planned for myself and this couldn't be what God wanted for my life, I thought.

Until one day, He revealed that it was surely apart of His plan for me. Struggling with how to cope and manage from day to day as my thoughts were rolling over one event to another, trying to figure it all out. Lord, I need your help was my plea; not knowing where to start or what to say. So I decided to seek God through fasting and praying to purge that which was clouding my view and hindering me from progressing. A time of cleansing to draw my mind, heart and spirit back to a place of commune with God.

This was the beginning of my transformation process to becoming empowered. Releasing myself to be a vessel worthy of being used to speak out and revealing how my brokenness was needed in order for me to rely more on God and not in my own strength or even that of a man. He used those situations to push me into His purpose for my life. There was more that He wanted from me. God allows us to be thrown into the pressures and storms of life to get us to a specific point of total dependency on Him. If He didn't do that we'd feel like we could handle things and never see the possibility in the impossible which is what He want us to see. Feelings of anxiety, isolation and oppression can be overwhelming and cloud our vision of whom God had made us to be, women of extraordinary rapport; not just a virtuous, victorious woman, but a phenomenal woman of God. The adversary has cunningly diminished our thoughts of self-worth, self-esteem and self-sacrifice to the point that we too often think of ourselves last. No one can take care of us, other than God, like or better than we can. We're persistent, persevering, and protected by God's love for us, His grace and mercy towards us and because of His promise to fulfill His purpose within us.

Many days I truly felt like the hemorrhaging woman (Mark 5:25-34) because of everything that I was going through. Just as she had been dealing with an issue for a lengthy time, so was I trying to balance two major life changing issues. Both having its own effects on my faith, family and finances. Feelings of isolation at work and worship because of what had taken place caused me to lose hope. For who would ever believe, after all this, was one chosen by God to do His work. Just like her we're faced with opposition or in this case a problem, something that is so great that we can't see in the physical how to overcome. Your faith will cause a sense of urgency that makes you very steadfast. It was not her personal issue that challenged her, but the crowd that would delay her. Nevertheless her persistence would drive her to fight through those hindrances to get that which she knew she would receive. Many times we know who we are in God and what He has already promised us, but we don't act like we know our place in Him. We allow opinions from others, lack of interest from others and road blocks to stop us. There is power waiting to be released into us, but because of distractions, some may never receive it. When she confessed and was willing to come forth with boldness to take a stand in her PLACE with Him, which He confirms as Daughter in the kingdom. What an example we have of attributes of a phenomenal woman:

-Persistent to the faith in which we must stand firm on

-Persevering through every obstacle, trial or persecution that comes our way

-Protected by the very promises God gives us to those who diligently seek Him first.

Daily I sought God's voice and direction until I heard him speak to me. Do you not know that the first step to moving forward is forgiveness? Forgiving those that have wronged you is not for them, but solely for you. Sometimes it may mean forgiving yourself for not making certain decisions sooner or for taking on others perceptions and opinions as your own. God requires that we forgive our offenders because we were once that same offender to Him and He died so that we could be forgiven. God revealed the importance of this very thing so that I could begin my transformation to healing. Standing firm on God's word, His promise and His power is what allows us to be separated from others to be the phenomenal woman of God that He has made us to walk in and live by. Relying on our faith, remaining faithful to what we believe and staying focused until we receive exactly what God said is already ours in His Word.

"God has transformed my tears into His testimony, my pain into His power and my words into His wisdom that others would see none of me, but All of HIM."

MEMOIR VII

CAROLE'S MEMOIR
LIFE EXPERIENCES

Jesus answered and said unto her, Whosoever drinketh of this water shall thirst again: But whosoever drinketh of the water that I shall give him shall never thirst; but the water that I shall give him shall be in him a well of water springing up into everlasting life." John 4:13-14 KJV

March 30, 1970 - That was the day I graced the world with my presence. Little did I know how tumultuous my life would turn out to be. I was born and raised in San Francisco. My father and mother were both immigrants from China and Hong Kong, respectively. They eventually had five children, but, at that time, there were only my two sisters and me. My younger sister and brother were born four and five years after me. While my mom was pregnant with me, she had rubella (German measles). So I was born completely blind in both eyes. Thank God for his first miracle in my life. The doctors operated and were able to give me sight in my left eye. I later learned that some babies born to mothers with rubella died and those who survived had disabilities that were much more severe than mine.

My parents were very old-fashioned and they placed more value on having sons than having daughters. I definitely sensed that during my childhood. To make matters worse, my father wasn't at home much and my mother had to bear the burden of raising all five of us, with little or no help from him. All that stress and frustration caused her to take things out on me and the fact that her own childhood had also been traumatic didn't help. Little things would set her off, such as me swallowing toothpaste instead of spitting it out.

When I was about three years old, I was removed from my parents' house and placed in foster care. I had to live in an emergency home until Child Protective Services found a more permanent placement for me. After about a year, I was placed with a Filipino family in the Hunter's Point neighborhood of S.F. I lived there for about five years. I visited my birth family on weekends. I didn't feel a part of either family though because I was definitely treated like an outsider in the foster home and I only saw my sisters and brother on weekends. I also felt different at school since I was the only student in foster care.

I soon found out that my father was dying of lung cancer and he wanted me back home. He passed away in November 1979 and I was returned to my mother. By then my family was living in the Bernal Heights neighborhood of the city, right near the Alemany housing projects, which was also known as "The Black Hole." We were one of only two Chinese families living in that neighborhood, which was predominantly Black and Latino. My siblings and I got into several fights with the kids in the neighborhood, who teased us because of our "strange" language.

Unfortunately my mother was still very physically and emotionally abusive. In addition to her abuse, I had to endure the abuse of my two older sisters, who had followed my mother's example. My sisters were also abusive to my brother. I saw and experienced much more violence in that house than I ever saw on TV or in the streets.

I suffered with the abuse until I decided to run away when I was twelve years old. Since I didn't really have anywhere else to go, I just wandered the streets until about midnight, when I finally got tired and went home. My mother answered the door and said, with no emotion at all, "If you hadn't come home, we would have called the police." That was the end of it and nothing else was ever said about the incident.

I had to put up with my dysfunctional family for a little while longer, until I was about sixteen years old. I went to school that day and I decided not to go back home afterwards. I had a male friend I met at summer camp and he let me stay with him for one night. After that, I went to stay with a woman I met through the S.F. Big Brothers and Big Sisters organization, a wonderful agency providing mentors to troubled youth. Since I was still a ward of the court, I was told that I could not live with someone other than my mother.

So I was placed in a group home for teenage girls, operated by the Charila Homes in S.F. They actually had three homes, dividing the girls by age. I ended up living in all three houses. However, when I was 17 years old, I got pregnant and I had to move to Florence Crittendon, another group home. This one was for pregnant teens and teen moms. On June 12, 1988, I gave birth to a beautiful and healthy baby girl, who weighed 8 lbs. and 2 oz.

Once I turned 18, I tried living with my mom and siblings again, but it didn't work out at all. So I moved out and I have been on my own ever since. I began taking classes at City College of S.F. and I was also volunteering at Juvenile Hall. Although I was doing fairly well in life, at that point, I was hanging around with the wrong crowd.

I had already started drinking, back when I was about 14 years old. I was mainly drinking Old English 800 malt liquor and I guess that was my favorite. In the late 1980's, I met a guy at this restaurant I used to go to all the time and he introduced me to crack cocaine. I heard some horror stories about people on crack. But this friend was a functional addict. He was able to go to work every day and he said he only smoked on weekends. So, at that point, I just thought the other people I heard about were just stupid for letting crack ruin their lives.

Fortunately, I didn't get hooked right away. I only did it occasionally. But, after the birth of my second daughter two years later, I began smoking a lot more. I was living in the Tenderloin, with my daughter and her stepfather. Crack was too readily available there. We didn't even have to leave the sixth floor to get some. Even the apartment manager smoked crack.

My addiction to crack lasted through all of the 1990's and I also had two more children during that time. My kids ended up living with a family member, while I tried desperately to get help with my addiction. I went through several drug treatment programs (both outpatient and residential), all to no avail. After being evicted from our apartment in the Tenderloin, we lived in several homeless shelters, in between rehab programs.

We finally got a three-bedroom apartment and we came close to having our son returned to us. The only setback was that the apartment was in the North Beach housing projects, which is all we could afford at that time. We only lived there for one year and it turned out to be worse than the five years we lived in the Tenderloin.

We were harassed by the kids in the neighborhood on a daily basis. There were plenty of drug dealers, some of whom had no qualms about breaking into our apartment, regardless of whether it was day or night and regardless of whether we were home or not. Neither the manager nor the police were much help at all. One of the teenagers told us that, at one point, they were thinking of firebombing our apartment. Thank God that never happened. When we first moved in, we had been clean for a little while. But, needless to say, we didn't stay clean because of the availability of the drug and the constant stress of trying to deal with all the harassment we experienced.

It was an extremely trying time in my life. I lost so much due to my addiction, including custody of my children, several places to live, and numerous material possessions. But it wasn't until I gave my life to Jesus in 1996, at the Richmond Rescue Mission, that I began to see a light at the end of the tunnel. I went through the last stage of my addiction and, finally in 1999, I got clean and stayed clean. I have been clean now for 12 years. HALLELUJAH!!! In 2001, I began taking classes in Criminal Justice at Contra Costa College. Then I transferred to S.F. State University in 2004. I received my Bachelor's Degree in Criminal Justice in 2008.

But, because the job market is so competitive, I felt that I needed something else, in addition to my degree. So I decided to try to get into law school. Unfortunately, that didn't happen because I couldn't get past the Law School Admission Test (LSAT). I was disappointed, but not for long. I soon registered for Paralegal classes at S.F. State University and I received my Paralegal Certificate in June 2011.

Unfortunately my family went through some major struggles during that time. Two of my cousins, Donte Boone and Travante James, and a good friend of mine from C.C. College, Keith Stephens, were all shot and killed in the Bay Area. All of the trauma motivated me to get involved in violence prevention. I am currently active with the Healing Circle for the Soul Support Group in S.F. and the Healing Circles of Hope in Richmond, both fully committed to stopping the violence and encouraging survivors to turn their pain into self-empowerment.

During the hard times, my trust in God was never very far away. I had been baptized back when I lived with my foster family and I was constantly praying for help throughout my addiction. My relationship with God got much stronger once I accepted God's help instead of trying to succeed on my own. I realized that I definitely could not have turned things around without HIS powerful hand guiding me.

In 2003, I found an excellent church in Berkeley, CA. Covenant Worship Center, under the very strong leadership of Pastor K.R. Woods, who is, by far, the most powerful house of God I have ever been to and I have been to several churches in my time. After my very first visit to CWC, I knew, immediately, that I wanted to become a member. CWC is definitely "A Church on a Mission" and I can easily see myself being a member for life.

MEMOIR VIII

CYNTHIA'S MEMOIR
GOD WHY?

"Many are saying of me, 'God will not deliver him. But you, LORD, are a shield around me, my glory, the One who lifts my head high."
Psalm 3:2-3 NIV

"God, why?" is the question I often ask. Sometimes I think where would my life be if things would've been different, if I had a normal childhood, adolescent and adult life.

I was introduced to sex early, around four years old, molested by my grandfather and a "friend of the family". Instead of wanting to play with Barbie dolls and toys I wanted to have a boyfriend, and a relationship. I had had sexual feelings and sexual thoughts that no young girl should have. "God Why?" I was pushed into adulthood at such a young age, instead of normal weekend activities of cheerleading, swimming etc. we were at my aunt's house to escape. My parents had a rough relationship. My dad was heavily on drugs and going to visit him in various jails was a routine. I am a daddy's girl and loved my daddy as much as my mom. I had hoped things would get better. Yet being exposed to drama and the idea that I was suppose to "hang in there" both helped and harmed me in relationships and throughout my life. Though I believe my parents did the best they could to raise me, my sister and brother. But my parents also had their own emotional scars from there childhood and hard lives.

At 11 yrs old, I had a turning period in my life. Most girls that age would be excited about being a pre-teenager soon; having that feeling of "I'm almost grown". But not me, I was wondering if I would live or die. I began to have seizures out of nowhere. My parents and doctors were baffled. I was a pretty healthy child besides episodes with asthma. The diagnosis: a brain tumor in the right temporal lobe of my brain. "God why?" No one talked to me about how I felt, the fear, the doubt, I asked God, "Why me? What did I do wrong? Would I end up like the persons on TV who wear a helmet? Would I need someone to help me do the basics such as personal care?" I had no one to talk about all these feelings, my parents were from the generation were the children's feelings didn't matter.

After the diagnosis, I became a lab rat. For months, doctors prescribed me every seizure medicine possible. Etched in my memory is the time I had a seizure in a retail store, which was the first time where I actually passed out. My mom was terrified, yet God sent an angel, a lady in the store to help me. It's amazing how God never left me. I remember being prepped for the brain surgery at a local children's hospital. I had fears, yet calm. I always sensed that God was with me even as a young girl. As they rolled me though the double doors, I was slightly sedated, yet God gave me a vision. In this vision, he showed me my life that it wouldn't end but go forward without struggle. Boy, did I have MANY struggles!

After a brain tumor removal I had to deal with a learning disability, emotional problems, constantly fighting for education, work accommodations and disability benefits. I've been fighting all my life "God, Why?"

I consider my teenage years as the worse years of my life. At thirteen years old I had already lost my virginity to a man 20 yrs old. He was what I considered "My first love". By sixteen years old, I graduated from drinking wine coolers to hard liquor, E & J and orange juice was my "favorite" choice. I was defiant and disrespectful. If I even thought you were "crossing the line" I would cut you, not with a knife, but I had a tongue and attitude that was deadlier then any physical weapon. From 13 yrs old until my mid-twenties was a period of darkness. It was the darkness of dealing with a learning disability. I had low self-esteem. I hated my dark skin and thick hair. I was tall and skinny with large feet. During the 1990's this was considered a curse. In the dark period, I had numerous sexual experiences with various men. I had the idea "The more I give the man the more he would love me; this stemmed from the molestation. I would be promised candy or engaged with my molester because that was a way to get attention, and I was often threatened with the infamous, "If you tell, no one will believe you".

I had twisted thoughts, I would often be the "seducer", I would literally go after men whom could care less about me. I had this idea I could save them; the same attitude my mom had towards my dad and the idea" If you stick it out he'll change". I was so fierce at using my seducing ways I received numerous jobs which I wasn't qualified for, "hook ups" and gifts, a Jezebel spirit. I stayed in numerous relationships and situations with men that were unhealthy. I have struggled with trust because I trusted the men who molested me and throughout my life I have been constantly hurt by people which has contributed to me being a introverted person God By my mid twenties, I said to myself enough is enough. I "fasted" from men and intimate relationships, there's a saying "You can believe you're delivered, but you're not FREE". And I wasn't, because I quickly reverted back to old habits after years of abstinence. When I reverted back this time, I figured if I have intimate relations with men, here and there, instead of frequently it would be better, right? No! it was much worse. Why? Because the longer you continue abusing yourself whether it's with drugs, food, or sex it can cause damage. When God says NO or STOP and you frequently disobey him, he'll get you to the point you'll have no choice but to say YES LORD!

I remember in my late twenties God spoke to me and said, "When is it going to be enough?" Though in my early twenties I said enough, but God wasn't in it. Unfortunately, after years of abuse, thinking I have to open myself physically and emotionally has caused significant internal damage from years of "experiences" and spiritual damage. So the question now, after all you been through what's next? REAL GOD relationship, once again I must say "You can believe you're delivered but you're not FREE". From a young girl, I was made to attend church out of ritual never taught about a real relationship with God. Just "Fake it 'til you make it". I also had a twisted view of relationships. I thought God was the same as the men I experienced in my past; that he couldn't truly love me. But, slowly and surely God is now taking my broken pieces and constructing it back together to wholeness. I've looked myself in the mirror and accepted who I am. Comfortable with my personal appearance, I also accepted that I have a learning disability but with determination and positive thinking I will succeed. I am no longer settling for ANYTHING or ANYONE that will lead to a dead end. Now I am moving forward in my true calling which is to help and inspire others with my testimony and to let them know regardless of life circumstances you can make it. The gifts of prophetic dreams, visions, singing and other gifts he has imparted within me since birth, I now accept. Am I perfect? NO! But I'm fighting to become what God wants me to be

MEMOIR IX

MYESHA GREEN
NOW I KNOW

Now I know that the LORD is greater than all gods: for in the thing wherein they dealt proudly he was above them." Exodus 18:11 KJV

"Would somebody help me please!!!?" Those were the excruciating words I heard my father, yell. I really didn't know that those would be some of the last words I would hear him say. We had to rush my father to the emergency room. The doctors discovered that he was having an intestinal reaction to a recent surgery, implanting a feeding tube. This was due to a tumor that was on his esophagus which caused him to have problems eating.

As a 15 year old child I didn't recognize the impact that this would have on me as an adult. I didn't know that the last moments with my father would be giving him medicine through a feeding tube; and these would be the last memories that I would have. Losing or not having a father around can make or break a child's future. I know because my life has been a struggle. At times I wasn't even aware of what could or would come. As I look back over my life, I realize why I did much of what I did. I didn't see it in the midst of it. But now that I'm older I can see beyond the surface of things.

When my father passed, I dealt with it by being very humorous and running away to another city. I goofed around with my family, not realizing that I was really avoiding the pain. I moved away to another city thinking that would solve what I was feeling, which was being alone. I tried to cover it by saying, "Yeah I'm strong and I'm going away to college". While on the inside, I was so hurt. Not only did I try to run away from it, I tried to find a substitute for it. I ran from relationship to relationship thinking that I was ok because I was sleeping around with these guys. But I was damaging my self-esteem. While in school, I wasn't focused, all I did was go out to the clubs and college parties and hang out. It wasn't until I experienced tremendous heart break from a relationship that drove me to my knees. This is when God first got my attention. I was so hurt and devastated. I stopped going to class as if I could afford to stop going. Soon thereafter I was kicked out of school.

For a while, I went around telling myself and others that school isn't for me or for everyone. But one day someone didn't accept that from me as an excuse. They told me that school was for me and that I could do it. After a long conversation with that person I began to give school a second thought. I couldn't go back to the CSU, so I enrolled in the junior college. It was a struggle for me because I knew I had more in me than where I was. But I stuck with the process. At first I wasn't doing very well. One Sunday morning, I heard my pastor say, as he was preaching, "Don't learn the material for the grade, learn the material to learn." That had the biggest impact on my studies. Once I grasped that concept, my grades and attitude towards school changed drastically. I began to have a different outlook on school. Now some might have already grasped that concept but this was coming from someone who was the first in their family to actually go away to college and break the norm of what had been. Although I didn't know this is what I was doing God knew all along.

Some people are fortunate enough to have someone come in and fill the void after losing a loved one, primarily their father. I wasn't. And if they were there I was so busy trying to run away and avoid the pain that I was unable to receive it. I didn't have anyone there to validate me as a normal father would. Nor did I have a father there to protect me from guys that were up to no good in my life. Many times I've felt that women and some men have mistaken my actions, thinking that I was flirting or something else. All I was doing was seeking a fatherly figure. I was looking for someone to fill the place of something that was involuntarily taken away from me. It is only by the grace of God that my life hasn't turned out worst.

According to society and statistics, I should have been dead by suicide, street violence, or an STD .

I'm not saying I don't have my struggles now because I still do , but when I look at the facts, I recognize that far more could have taken place in my life. I have struggled with my self-esteem on a great level. As mentioned before I didn't have my father around to validate who I was, I would accept all types of abusive behavior from people. Although I have never been physically abused, I've been verbally abused.

Once my father died I had freedom to do whatever. Then I left and went away to school thinking I was grown. I've had many people tell me that moving to a city where I had no family was brave of me. Truth is I didn't know what I was getting myself into, but God knew. I thought I was grown and didn't know I needed the help of others. So then now I struggle in my relationships with authority and with God at times. Although I'm better at it now I've had problems submitting to authority. Not that I didn't want to its just something I wasn't used to. I didn't know how to respond to strong figures in my life due to the fact that I was so used to doing things on my own.

Having to teach yourself to do things and then be criticized and talked about for doing so is not the best thing. I know life is a struggle but who am I to judge my struggles against yours. Some people didn't realize what it was like to walk in my shoes and tried to handle it accordingly.

At the time of my father's death, I didn't grieve or mourn. I recall having to be strong for my mother and sister. They took this death to the core of their hearts. My mom always said "when they made your dad, they broke the mode." My father meant everything to my mom and I believe they had something quite special. At his time of death they were married for 13years. It wasn't until maybe 3 years ago that I began the process. I would cry and not know why I was crying. We then had a grievance class taught at church and that's when I realized what was going on with me. It seemed like all the pieces came together at that point. I understood myself and some people around me better.

With my entire struggle, it is now my desire to create a program for those that are fatherless. I believe this is one of the main reasons for the problems in society. There is a lack of fathers in the home, or kids not having a stable home environment. I don't want to offend anyone but this is just my opinion from my personal experience. I truly believe if we can provide a safe haven for our youth, society would be different. We wouldn't have young girls running around with half their body showing and feeling like sex or the attention from a young man equals love. The young men also need strong male role models to show them what a real father and man is. This is the original plan of God, two parents, a mother and father, a stable home environment. The man is there to provide guidance, structure, and authority in the home.

MEMOIR X

STEPHANEY'S MEMOIR
TO GOD BE THE GLORY

"And, ye fathers, provoke not your children to wrath: but bring them up in the nurture and admonition of the Lord."
Ephesians 6:4 KJV

I wanted to share with you all, this particular testimony that goes back in time. I pray that it encourages somebody that may be in need.

My name is Stephaney Hill. I am now 41 years old. My parents separated when I was about 14 years old and I stayed with my mother as opposed to moving out with my father. I remember him being heavily into drugs and being very financially irresponsible. I had always felt that my dad didn't do much with me or for me. It always seemed like mom did it all. I don't recall any piggy back rides, or daddy daughter talks or any one on one time spent with him. I do remember him being a coach for many years and coaching my brother's football teams. In fact that's all I remember is football, basketball or baseball conversations from my father and not much more. It was all about sports back then. Prior to the separation, one day I asked him to buy me an article of clothing. He said go ask your mom. However, when I heard my brother ask him for some socks I remember them going to the store and purchasing the socks. I figured, maybe mama provides for the girls and daddy provides for the boys. I thought "okay!"

By the time my parents separated, due to dads' infidelity, I was already sad and disappointed in him for not helping my mother financially and not fulfilling the promises he had made to his children. My mother carried a lot of the weight for the family and that wasn't right. I can't speak for my siblings and how they felt but this is what I was feeling as a 14 year old little girl.

A few years went by and I became pregnant at the age of 17. I was a junior in High School. Mom, made too much money at work, so I didn't qualify to receive any help through the public assistance program. I wouldn't become eligible until my 18th birthday. I wasn't getting much assistance from my baby's father. He was also a teenager at the time.

Rock cocaine was a popular drug back in the late 1980's and instead of seeking employment, I chose to sell drugs for fast money, to provide for myself and my baby, while still trying to finish High School. I picked up some bad habits and began to smoke marijuana and drink alcohol prior to getting pregnant, but I was smart enough to take a break from the drugs and alcohol during my pregnancy. Praise the Lord!

There were some family members that wanted to buy drugs from me but I would not sell to them. However, I did sell drugs to some of their friends. The enemy had me all twisted up because when my dad came to me wanting to buy drugs, I sold them to him with the attitude that "this is the only way I'm going to get any money out of him". That went on for a couple of years. I felt no shame or guilt whatsoever; in fact I was adamant about selling him the drugs. The anger had built up so strong that I had lost a lot of respect for my father at this point in my life and didn't know exactly how to feel about him.

I knew that a part of me still loved him but my anger towards him had taken over. I always knew to pray, and I would ask God to help my father with his drug addiction, but I didn't ask for much help for myself. I thank God for the friends and family members that were praying for me. All my life I have had a praying grandmother. I know that God answered her prayers which have helped make a difference in me.

I stand before you today to say that, I am living proof that God is a forgiver and a deliverer, hallelujah! I have been clean from marijuana for 4 years now and I can honestly, pick up the phone, call my father and have a decent conversation with him, without any hard feelings. I love him just like I love my mother. Our family celebrates Father's Day every year by having a big reunion. This past Father's Day, June 19, 2011, we celebrated the 12th year. My dad is there most of the time and he evens calls me on Mother's Day now to wish me a happy Mother's Day. It feels so good to be forgiven and delivered from such strongholds that the enemy loves to hang over our heads. I have been set free.

Today, I am a Sunday School Teacher, the head of our Single's Ministry at my church, the proud mother of two boys and a daycare owner (5 yrs), and I've been born again since August 24, 2008. Thank you Jesus!

Do not ever give up on your fathers, even if you feel neglected or disowned because you never know what God is up to. The battle is truly, not ours, it's the Lords. Remember it's his will that we want to live in and not our own. If you don't have the spirit of forgiveness, ask God for the help and he will be there to see you through. With a crushed heart, anger, un-forgiveness, and some bad habits, I made it! Glory be to God.

MEMOIR XI

TAHISHA'S MEMOIR
MY LIFE I LOVE

"Have not I commanded thee? Be strong and of a good courage; be not afraid, neither be thou dismayed: for the LORD thy God is with thee whithersoever thou goest" Joshua 1:9 KJV

God is a great God. I'm 22 yrs old and I don't even look like what I've been through. Born May 4th 1989 by a beautiful woman whom arms I never felt again until I was 13yrs old. Why? My mother had a drug addiction, so my dad took me from her at the age of 3 and then left me with his girlfriend who took care of me until I left her house at 18. My father was abusive to my second mother so he was in and out of my life. Not once when they fought did he take me or even come and talk to me one on one... we never had the father daughter relationship most of my friends have. I was hurt, lost, confused, and abandoned.

Every day before I was 13 and even after I cried myself asleep longing for my mom... it's amazing how I knew my second mother was not my first mother, as well as I knew my sister was not my blood...how? They were lighter and my dad and I were darker then I got older and found out the truth...See its hard to be raised by a family that u know is not your blood and you're constantly longing for someone to come and take u back home. For years, I wanted someone, anyone to just come and say they were a family member and they've come to take me back home; but it never happened.

At the age of 13, I was no longer a virgin or pure as some people would say. My dad was not there to teach me to wait until I was married and my mother was on drugs somewhere... so I did what I wanted and didn't care who I hurt because everyone else had hurt me. After I had sex for the first time, I went from being an honor roll student to an average student and I had the worst temper. I threatened to kill people, fought until I seen blood and kept all my pain inside. Yea I could've gone to my second mother. But why would I want to hurt her with my pain when she took me in when she didn't have to? How selfish of me to even put her through that.

I started to write poems and keep journals after reading a book by Maya Angelou who was my only role model. So I'm writing, revealing the hurtful things I'm being faced with; not only was I sexually active with both males and females, I was suicidal. I would go into the kitchen while everyone was asleep, take the knife into the bathroom and press it into my stomach or wrist. Every time I would do this I would cry and say "God help me".

Now at this time I had no real relationship with Christ. My dad is a Muslim and even though that was only practiced during Ramadan, there was no real practice of any religion for that matter. One thing I clearly remember is always looking out to the stars and praying and asking God to protect my mother and other siblings and to get me back to her. Now understand my second mother did the best she could but I WANTED MY BIRTH MOTHER. I wanted her so badly I would run away for hours and even overnight leaving my second mom in pain and worrying. No it was not right but I wanted what I wanted. Every night when I looked out to the stars I would pray, pray for a way out.

I had other siblings who I lived with; I loved them but I did not want to be there. We would argue and fight; like siblings do but as we got older I didn't like it. I was very fond of my two younger brothers. When I started working, I would take them shopping with me and give them whatever I could afford. One of them, who is now 17, was like my best friend; he and I were so close. He always called me a nerd; we played basketball together, watched wrestling together, and only had one fist fight. This one fight stuck in my mind because he and I both cried; he being the second to the youngest was the man of the house. But we both displayed characteristics of our dad that showed how alike we were. After graduation, I gave him everything I couldn't take. Whenever I'd come home to visit, though he was younger than me he would pick me up and swing me around like I was the little sister. Many of my experiences with my siblings meant a lot to me, but our relationship made me love my brothers and sisters unconditionally and it filled the gap where I was still empty.

At the age of 15, my mother died from domestic violence. Whether some people chose to believe it or not, my mother was clean from drugs and had been for a while. Before she died, she and I talked almost every day and I couldn't wait to get home from school and call her or she would call me. I would talk, laugh and ask questions about why she could never come get me; I wanted to know everything about her and what she had been through. Days had gone by and then months, of her and I talking for hours. I never wanted to get off the phone; I wanted to be close to her and I didn't care what it took to do that. My life started to change the more we talked; the most important thing to change was I started feeling better about who I was. and I no longer had so much pain and anger. My relationship with my second mother started to change. I could see how one can feel threatened or feel intimated when something has always been with you, may be leaving.

<u>A Phenomenal Woman IV</u>

By: Lady Elder Bessie Sims

A Woman of Beauty

When she walks into a room her radiance is as beautiful as the tropical sun; her silhouette glows with grace and you can see the blessings flowing with her pace, while the anointing continue to shine on her face; Yes , she had her battles, and oh yes she has won – the battles scars are proof of the victories she has won; Her ambition is contagious, her uniqueness is so outrageous and oooooh she is so amazing; you can say she is a powerful outstanding woman and all; Oh yes , she is a beautiful woman taking this journey because she was called; there is beauty in her strength to keep her soul in shape with God; there is beauty in her flaws that help her realize how she has evolved knowing that with every mistake God still loves her even when she falls; the beauty of her tears that fuels the transportation to get her through the years – this is her journey of beauty that has made her strong?

She is a Woman of Beauty – a Phenomenal Woman Soaring through it all!

MEMOIR XII

LATOYA'S MEMOIR
CHAPTER OF CHANGE

"May you experience the love of Christ, though it is too great to understand fully. Then you will be made complete with all the fullness of life and power that comes from God."
Ephesians 3:19 NLT

The pivotal moment in my life was the day I had a freak accident which kept me from attending my first semester of college. During this season of my life I was battling with several different issues from rebellion to sexual identity crisis. I was a woman who was empty and lonely. I can remember growing up "hearing" about God, but not "knowing" God. I could never forget this specific moment of my life because it was the moment that led to my father's death and changed my life forever.

I was riding down an incline on rollerblades when I realized the breaks had been removed. With force, I flew into a parked truck. I can see the lights and hear the sound of the ambulance as if it were yesterday. After arriving to the hospital and undergoing several x-rays, I braced myself as I prepared to hear the word surgery. This was such a devastating moment, especially after all the plans that I had made for my first year experience of college. I was going to do everything my dad would not let me do. I was ready to move away from my parents to experience what I called "FREEDOM." As I returned home, I realized I would be at home with my father, where the relationship just was not the best. Stuck there for six months with a man I had grown to dislike, NO! I did not want to be there.

In exchange for my dad's presence, I chose pain pills. Pain pills and sleep became my best friend for several months. During those several months, I looked for my "best friend" to take me away forever. I had never experienced such a dark moment in my life such as this. I could not understand why I felt so lonely, depressed and insignificant. Even if I wanted to try the God thing, I could not because I was still trying to figure out how everyone else was putting so much trust in Him. I wanted a quick fix. I needed something that would take all my hurt away and change my life forever. God, no there were just too many questions.

Finally after months of pills and sleep, my wish of getting off to college had arrived. Never did I imagine after so much excitement of leaving home, I would be receiving a call to inform me of my father's massive heart attack. Things begin to change for me; my path of darkness became greater. The loneliness and depression increased. I felt that only person I had to run to was the same girl I had been dating which brought total separation between me and my family. It did not matter, because I thought this was "real" love.

Living in a dark place and seeking love in all the wrong places, led me once again to a place of wanting to take my life. I was burdened with so much guilt and shame. The one father, who I had grown to dislike, suddenly changed to a heart of love. My life was in total chaos. I never had the chance to tell my dad I was sorry for all my rebellious and hateful ways. It was not easy to be stuck with guilt and the thought of it being too late to ask for forgiveness.

In 2002, a year that will never be forgotten, something extremely powerful took place. As I was rolling over one morning to get ready for class, I experienced a feeling and to this day, I still cannot explain. This was the beginning of a life transformation. Suddenly, I could see things clearly and differently. My darkness has been turned into light. It seemed as if I had just snapped from a horrible dream. I unapologetically released everything from friends to music, in order to pursue this new craving. I was led to pick up a Bible for the first time in my life. In solitude for almost 2 years I lived, breathed, and ate 1 Corinthians 13.

For someone who had so many questions and had no desire to seek a relationship with the Lord has now been changed forever. God took me from a place of depression, self-doubt, fear, negativity, loneliness, and low self-esteem into a place of strength and confidence. After being afraid that I would never gain my reputation back, He restored it all.

Now when I look back over my life, I realize that even through my rebellious ways and negative thoughts, God had His hands on me through it all. I have never known a love so strong and overwhelming until I experienced His divine love. For a while I lived in fear of sharing and being open with my past because I was afraid of how others would view or judge me. While reflecting back on my season of the sexual identity crisis, I can remember it being the most sensitive to me because I did not think that I would ever find a special someone that would love me sincerely regardless of my past. Who would want to fall in love with someone such as myself that had been so torn apart? I stand today truly thankful and blessed that God had things already prepared for me. After learning to totally trust and learn His ways, I can now smile with confidence knowing He had everything under control.

I am now married to an amazing man of God with two beautiful and healthy daughters, Hailey and Kalyn. Every day I am just overwhelmed with joy. I thank God for choosing a sinner like me, one that rejected Him and His love, to be a witness of His grace and mercy. When I should have been taken out by this world, He said NO! God knew in advance that there was purpose planted on the inside of me and the enemy could not have me. Although I feel so unworthy at times, I am forever blessed to be used by God. After all the times I rejected Him, He still loves me enough to use me. There is no longer a doubt in my mind about the power of God. He is my healer, refuge, comforter, and the lover of my soul. This love can never be replaced and no one could ever compare to the love I have received from my Heavenly Father. My worries have been removed, doubts have been erased, and the negative thoughts have been destroyed. I now see through the eyes of God, understanding that He has the provision for my life. Through all the past trials and tribulations I have faced, he has been with me, giving me strength that will allow me to endure this present season. God has been working in my life by proportions, considering my weakness and faintheartedness. Although life will constantly throw unexpected blows, I have learned to place total confidence and trust in the Father. I have found rest in the love and promises of God.

Every encounter that I have faced has prepared me for this very moment, even when I did not know it. Every situation was God's disguised training. I am now, not only a career woman, but the First Lady of Church of the Champions in Grambling, La. I am a living testimony that God is real and His love for all of His children is breath taking. It is amazing how I never saw myself as beautiful and now I stand with boldness to proclaim the Gospel of Jesus Christ. I am a strong believer that "love" is the greatest gift locked inside of each and every individual. Through ever dilemma I have faced in life from the past to this present moment, they have molded and developed me to fit God's divine purpose for my life. In the midst of overcoming my challenges, God truly stepped in and redirected my life in a way I never imagined.

My encouragement to women now is that God can and will provide a way out. No matter how messed up we may think we are, God still only can see the beauty and potential of His marvelous creation. Our Heavenly Father's desire for us is to experience a life of abundance. We, as women, must understand that God has a plan for our lives. We are part of His divine plan and we are made in His image. We are God's precious jewels, His chosen ones. It is time that we release the pain and fears of our past and begin to see ourselves though the heart of God. Know that we have royal blood running through our veins. God loves you and longs to have an intimate and authentic relationship with us. We are conquerors and victorious.

I strive daily to reach as many women as I can through my life style of serving, love, and faith. My mission is the help women, along with others, realize the power that love has in their lives. Although there have been set backs, heartaches, several disappointments, I pray that women all around the world know that it's not too late to become all that God desires her to be. I thirst for women to experience the same love encounter so that they may be restored, healed, made whole by the love of God and know they are the sparkle of His eye. Ephesians 3:19 NLT says, "May you experience the love of Christ, though it is too great to understand fully. Then you will be made complete with all the fullness of life and power that comes from God."

May we all embrace the fact that we are valuable even in the midst of the trials we are facing right now. God understands that the pressures of life are critical to developing the shape of our future. We serve a magnificent and loving God. His love for each of us is everlasting and endures forever. As I open myself up to you and reveal the powerful works of our Heavenly Father, I pray you also pursue the same love experience. It will come with many tears and a great amount of sacrifice, but this is an experience that is priceless. My challenge is that you no longer dwell on the past but press forward into a bright, beautiful and promising future. No matter what background you come from, God is waiting to shower you with His compassion and unconditional love.

MEMOIR XIII

SHANICE'S MEMOIR
THEY CALL ME RUTH

Now I know that the LORD is greater than all gods: for in the thing "And Ruth said, Intreat me not to leave thee, or to return from following after thee: for whither thou goest, I will go; and where thou lodgest, I will lodge: thy people shall be my people, and thy God my God:" Ruth 1:16 KJV

Ruth initially represented 3 things for me, sacrifice, obedience, and hard work. I see myself as Ruth, Naomi as Jesus, Moab as the world and Judah as a life in Christ. On the surface, when I first read the book of Ruth, I felt her story was my story. Our lives started the same, her journey is the journey I'm currently on, and her end is the future I hope for.

A typical black girl from the hood is the life I lived. I came from a single parent home, unsure of who my father was. I had no identity. Growing up as a teen, I searched for a missing piece of me and didn't even know what was missing. I was truly a product of the world. So I searched and gave myself away, piece by piece, in hopes I'd find that one piece to complete me. At the age of 21 I was married. I thought I had found that piece, but in reality I had given the last of me away. One year later I had a son. Less than a year after that, I was divorced.

It was typical, why would I expect anything different for my life. My great grandma was a single mother who begot a single mother, who begot my mother, who begot me..... A single mother. The one thing I dreaded the most was happening to me. I never wanted a child to be as empty as I was right at that moment.

Like Ruth I had lost my husband, not to death but to another woman. Nevertheless he was gone. Ruth sacrificed; she left her home, her family her friends. She left a place where life could have been easy for her; to move to a place filled with work. She worked hard, early morning to evening. She obeyed the instruction Naomi gave her.

I didn't grow up in church, so I rarely prayed. I remember when I was young, my grandmother, a praying woman, taught me and my cousin how to pray. She also told us when we were fearful, felt troubled, or alone we should call on the name of Jesus. I remember the night I cried out his name, my whole life changed.

I sacrificed. I chose to take care of my sick mother-in-law. I chose to continue the duties I performed for her while I was married to her son.

I never turned my back on his family; my family. And in the midst of all of this, I also found a church home. I remember going to the altar broken and all I ask God to do was to heal the pain in my heart and help me to forgive. He told me to invite to church those who hurt me and whom I wanted to forgive. He told me to share his goodness with them. At first I was crushed, this was the one place I could find my peace of mind. This comfort, love, and simply a place I could get away from the world. God, you want me to share this place with those who bring pain to my heart with every beat? I sacrifice my sacred place to obtain some inner peace.

Not only did I sacrifice, I was obedient to his word. I invited my ex-husband and his then fiancé to church. They didn't come at first, but I invited them until they showed up. My heart skipped a beat the moment they walked into the church doors. My flesh said "the enemy is in the building, time to show out". But my spirit said, "Go love them". (Pause: Now this is the man who left me and my son for the now pregnant woman who was standing beside him. God, you want me to do what? ....Play) When it was altar call time I went over and asked them to go with me to pray. They both looked at each other like I was crazy. We went and prayed and I ask God to release me right then and there. I don't know what the intercessor said to them, but I could hear God say to me "Freedom". I continued to invite them to church. Before I knew it I was sharing the Gospel with the both of them. Finally they joined the church. I called and reminded them about service every week. I even picked them up once or twice, just so they could get to service on time. For their wedding gift I got them a Couple's Bible. I would watch their children so they could go out and my son could spend time with his brothers. All the time it never dawned on me that everyone around me thought I was crazy for even interacting with them in such a personal way. God had entered my life and given me a forgiving heart to the point I did all those things without thought. I wouldn't say that we didn't share other ups and downs. I still had issues with their parenting habits toward my son, or should I say lack thereof. But I still served God's children like he asked me.

I also worked hard. Like Ruth, I had no support from a husband. I had a job, and I went to school. And I took care of my family (my son and anyone else I could assist.). After 3 long years in school, I graduated from Laney College receiving my AA in Social Science and Liberal Arts. I was accepted to five different universities. I finally choose to uproot, step out on faith, obey God and attend Grambling State University. I too moved away from my family, friends, and life as I knew it. For me it was another level of sacrifice, and deeper level of obedience, and a lot more hard work. This time the hard work is not only school, but also for the Lord.

Ruth chose to sacrifice, obey, and work hard, but not without guidance, she had a mentor. Ruth followed the advice of Naomi her mother in-law. Naomi was a woman of God and Ruth followed that spiritual guidance. Naomi told her the safe place to gather left over wheat and barley in the fields. She instructed her on how to approach Boaz. I, too, have a had Naomi in my life. My first Naomi was Lady Elder Bessie Sims. Elder Sims represented the family/ministry life, I desired. She was once a single mom and she struggled. She came to God and everything began to change for her. She even married a man of God who was also a single parent. They have a beautiful blended family, full of love.

When I first came to God, I didn't think anyone would want to marry me. I was divorced, already had a child and just all around tainted. But God led me to her, and I was shown that with Christ everything is possible. And once I came to Christ I was indeed a new creature. So I followed Bessie up until I left California. When I traveled to Louisiana, I could just imagine the fear of the unknown Ruth might have felt leaving Moab to go to Judah. This is what I felt as I left my home to go to someone else's land. When I arrived God assigned me a new Naomi, Latoya Tolbert. She represents the type of woman I need to become to be able to get, keep, and handle the family/ministry life I desire. She has truly been grooming me into that Proverb 31:10-31 woman Ruth was. She challenges me to embrace my calling, as well as how to take care of my first ministry, my Family. She's my guide, she teaches me how to love, to be humble and submissive. When the things in Ruth's life turned upside down, she could have turned back to her Moab ways, she could have stayed in that place. But instead she chose to follow Naomi, her protector, adviser, and guide. She went off to a new place with the promise of a better life, but it didn't come without sacrifice. She had to leave everything she knew and go into unfamiliar territory and trust Naomi the whole way. Much like my life with Christ it was some family and friends I had to leave behind, not to mention a whole state. I follow after the guidance of Christ. I sacrificed in order to live a better life. Ruth never questioned Naomi's advice and because of her sacrifice and her obedience she was blessed with everything the world stole from her and more.

In my Ruth story I'm still doing field work. I'm still hard at work at school and for God. I'm still being obedient still clinging to my Naomi. So my story isn't quite over, I have full faith that my Boaz is near. I know I will have everything restored to me, plus even more. So I continue to obey God's word, allow him to lead me, and trust him without any question.

MEMOIR XIV

OMIE'S MEMOIR
HIS GRACE AND MERCY
BLESSED ME WITH A NEW LIFE

For this is what the LORD says; You were sold for nothing
And without money you will be redeemed

Isaiah 52: 3 AMP

*"What we tend to overlook, when we are first attracted to butterfly observation, is that the butterfly is the result of a much longer journey......a journey that is quite different from that of many creatures on this planet." (**Stages of butterfly Development: Life Cycle of a Butterfly http://home.cogeco.ca/~lunker/stagesbf.htm**)*

The Lord came to me showing me myself in a metaphoric way as a butterfly. A butterfly represents three phases metaphorically in our Christian belief, the first phases Is as a caterpillar, the second phases is as a pupa and the third is the blooming of a butterfly. Through my journey, I have been through my own phases. He took me out of the poverty In Africa trough the "beautiful" mess in Sweden then to the Land of opportunities America, to then deliver me out of the curse in to he's Kingdom were I have always belonged In he's Love & Truth that concurs everything to tell me that he has always been with me before the foundation of he's creation he was with me and I with him hallelujah to GOD be the glory.

Omie Garba that's my name, I was born June 2, 1986 in a small West African country Republic of Gambia.

With the population of 1.7million where the dominating Religion is Islam I remember a lot of nature culture and color, as a child I remember being nurtured by my siblings on my father side and neighbors but never truly nurtured by my own mother such as a butterfly.

When I turned five I moved to Sweden to live with my mother and my siblings I'm the middle of four I have two younger sisters and two older brothers. As the oldest daughter of my single mother much was required of me. In my teen years I found myself taking care of my younger sisters cleaning and cooking and help my mother who was working a lot to put food on the table.

When people hear Sweden, they often think about a problem free country. That is in many ways true; however it can be very tough for a single mother with five kids and one income. For some reason we happened to do a lot of moving. It seemed like every time I got new friends and started feeling at home, it was time to move. When I first moved to Sweden in 1991, my mother was with a man who introduced to us the Swedish lifestyle and culture. On summer times, we would do a lot of camping and fishing by the Swedish country side. I remember the fresh air, the beautiful red cabins along the road; not to mention the Swedish flag with the bleu and yellow that represents the sky and the sun. Yes that's Sweden to me.

I remember one summer we went on a trip to our summer house (sommar stuga) as it's called in Swedish. Me my mother and my sibling decided to go to the beach and enjoy the beautiful weather. It was so hot that day, so my mother told me to go to the house and get the sun screen. Little did I know that would come to be one of the most horrible summers in my life? The man that I had come to like and looked up to as a father figure molested me that summer; I refused to take my eyes off the blue beautiful Swedish summer sky as the tears were streaming down my cheeks. I was so terrified to tell my mother what had happened, so I grabbed the sun screen and walked down to the beach and pretended like nothing ever happened.

After that summer, nothing was ever beautiful to me anymore. I became the greatest pretender. I could pretend that I was happy when deep down inside I was a lost black little girl even though I had my family around me I always felt alone as if a stranger in a strange land. As a child I can remember being attacked by the enemy in all kind of ways at that time I did not know why and what that was about. I was attacked in my dreams, at school and even at home. I wanted to disappear and never come back, but where would I go? No one knew what I was going through. I found myself talking to myself, saying that one day I was going to pack my bags and leave. By the age of fifteen It was time to move again and things started to get really bad at home. One of my brothers started to use drugs and got involved in criminal activities and that started to affect the whole household. It was around that time that I developed bulimia and anorexia. Everything around me was getting out of control and the only way I thought I could have some control was by controlling my body weight. I used to tell myself, if I can control my weight I would be the one in control then everything would be fine. That was all just a lie. This sickness followed me all through high school. It was not until I moved to America that God started to heal me. I found myself going to the gym and working out more even to this day. I'm fighting it by working out and eating right. Now I have a greater understanding to why I was being attacked in that way. God later revealed to me that I'm stronger when I'm in fasting mode and when my diet and body are in balance.

My mother started working for a Christian company called Open hand (Open hand) it was a big second hand company that helped people who lived in countries in poverty all over the world. My mother's supervisor happened to be the owner and the pastor of a church. He and his wife would invite us to service at their church. For some reason I started to like going to church, I could hear God speaking to me through the pastor.

One day me my mother and my sisters were in the kitchen, cooking. My mother cut a potato in half and as she did, we saw a cross inside it was as if someone had cut the potato in advance carved a cross inside of it and then glued it back together. Until this day I still think to myself how is that possible? But I know now that God speaks to us in different ways.

After junior high things started to change my mother met a man that would soon come to be her husband and we ended up moving again this time to the big city, Stockholm, the capital of Sweden. I remember thinking to myself, "Great now I can pursue my dream in becoming a musician in the big city. So I applied to a three year music program and my major was modern soul as it was called. I graduated 2005, my dream was to become a music artist, travel, and see the world. Due to six months of winter in Sweden, I decided I wanted to travel. My first destination was London and then New York. When I visited America for the first time I fell in love. It felt like home for some reason. It felt like the place I had tried to runaway to since I was a young girl. I told my friends when it was time to go home that they could go ahead and go back home without me I was ready and willing to find a way to stay but as ***Ecclesiastes; 3 says there is a***

***time for everything* .** I know now that the time was not yet there for me to fly.

So I went back home and signed up with the agency called cultural care au pair who sends out people from all over the world to work for American families in cultural exchange. As a newly graduated 20 year old I was ready to explore the world. I was ready for America. Little did I know that through my life's journey, this was soon going to become the part of my journey that I was going to meet my Creator.

I was first placed with a family in San Francisco due to the late night partying. In San Francisco's night life, we were known as the Scandinavian party girls among the inner circle of football and basketball players. We used to party Sunday to Sunday. After a couple of months the agency moved me to a family in a gated community in Orange County, it was during that time that the Lord took the alcohol. I started to receive dreams from the Lord and it was around that time, that I started to hear from the Lord more and more. When I turned 21years old, I gave my life to Jesus Christ. Little did I know that I had to get baptized and filled with the Holy Spirit and then find a church home. After six months living and working for the family in Orange County I decided to move back to the Bay area and start studying. I noticed how my dreams and goals started to change. My plan became to start school and then graduate as a Interior designer, by the age of 25 start my own company. I wanted to live the American dream and then fly back and forth to Sweden, and do business all over the world.

I studied two semesters at College. In my second semester, I got in contact with a psychic lady during a Jazz festival who told me that someone In my mother's family had put a Voodoo curse on me and my family and she even told me that I was the one to brake the curse and she was going to help me. During that time I was a baby In Christ. I did not know the word of God good enough to recognize the Devil. In three years, I gave all my student financial aid to this lady, thinking that I was doing the will of God. I was living in darkness being deceived controlled and manipulated. I started to lose everything, my apartment friends and even myself.

The psychic lady told me that I could not tell anyone or else it could not be broken. I know now that it was the trick of the devil to keep me in bondage. I saw all of my friends graduating and moving back to Sweden while I was falling deeper in to a dark world. I was not able to continue my studies because of the stress and spiritual warfare that I was in. I was not able to focus in class. All I could think about was to start working so that I could give her more money. **Leviticus19:26** warn us about divination sorcery and magic charms. I was so open to these things without knowing it because I had not yet received the holy spirit of God who leads and guides us into all truth.

My American dream turned in to my worst nightmare. I think that had I got baptized and filled with the Holy Spirit when I confessed my sins to Jesus and accepted him as my Lord and Savior back in Orange County, I would have not got so lost. Nevertheless God was always with me, watching over me helping, feeding and clothing me, everyday.

In two and a half years, I found myself couch hopping from home to home. Sometimes I would spend the night at the gym. In 2008 I meet a girl who told me about Covenant Worship Center because I was looking for a church. After I went there once, I knew in my heart that the presence of the Lord was there. Because I did not have stability then, I did not want to become a member. So for two years I would church hop. Every time I came to covenant, I would wear my cap and sit all the way in the back. It would be gone right before service was over because I did not want anyone to know me. I could not take the risk. One day at Covenant Worship Center, they asked if anyone wanted to become a member. For some reason I signed up after that I started going more and more. I wanted to seek God and know him more, but it felt like every time I got stronger In the Lord, I would fall into sin. I came in contact with a woman at the church who God later used to help me back home to he's His kingdom.

I started to go to San Jose on the weekends where the psychic lady lived to help her pass out flyers. I had no problem helping her because I thought she was sent to me by God to help me and my family. I later got a weekend job there, so that I could go and hand out flyers in the morning, before it was time to go to work. So now I was not able to go to Covenant Worship Center, anymore. One Sunday morning, I had to go to some mall and hand out flyers. I ended up at the Great Mall in San Jose to hand out flyers there. I did not know that I was going to run in to my friend from Covenant. By handing her one of the flyers without recognizing who I was giving it to. (She said Omie you will not die early) that is a saying in wolof (African language) when you see someone you just talked about. She then told me that my care pastors at church had just asked about me the same morning.

Little did I know that this was the beginning of my deliverance, the following Sunday God started to speak to me. He opened my spiritual eyes and allowed me to see in the spirit what was really going on in my life. He speaks to me in many different ways. I got myself a book because I felt like I needed to start writhing again. As I started to write, I was writing as if God was speaking directly to me. It went something like this, "Omie what happened to you? You used to be fun-loving, caring and out going, you used to love being around people. It is not you, it is that old lady. She is trying to steal your life. She does not want to live and does not want you to live.

As I was done writing, I started to read the words that I had written. I knew right away who the old lady was. God started to show me the mess that I was I could not stop myself from crying. The fear that came up on me was so heavy, I started to sweat. I had start smoking cigarettes it cumulated to two packs a day and instantly he removed that addiction.

On Wednesday I started a fast that God directed me to do. I decided that I was going to Bible study at Covenant Worship Center. I was speaking in tongues, all the way to church. As soon as I came into the church building, the song, "I know the Plans I Have for you" was on and I knew right away that it was the Lord speaking to me.

After service I kept hearing in my spirit, ask about baptism. So I did and on that day I was baptized November 14 2010 that was the beginning of my deliverance. He called me to fast all through the Thanksgiving weekend. And for each day I gained more and more insight in the spiritual realm. He told me to get rid of everything and anything that was given to me by that psychic lady, so I did. On the day of Thanksgiving I started to feel terrorized, as if some one was trying to kill me I could not explain to anyone what was going on in my body and mind. So I took my Bible with me and my telephone and start walking down the streets of Berkeley. I called my friend from church and she came and picked me up. I spent the night at her house. I could not sleep all night, because every time I would close my eyes, I would see horrifying things. I thought that I was going to die that night. I was being tormented in my mind by the enemy. I kept waking my friend up over and over again and she told me that I needed to get some help. If someone had seen me like this, they would take me to a mental hospital. I agreed with her that I was going to go to church in the morning as soon as the morning came. I took my bags and went to Covenant Worship Center. I felt in my spirit if I could make it to church, I would be fine. Without knowing if anyone was there or not I went to the front door and it was locked. I start praying, "Lord if it is your will, please makes a way". As soon as I was finished praying, I started to walk to the back side of the church. As I came into the church, I saw some people praying. This was on a Friday noon day prayer. The pressure, torment, and attacks in my mind body and soul made me feel like the devil was really trying to kill me. I walked over to the baptism pool and start speaking out loud saying to the enemy you are trying to take my life!!! I might as well die for Jesus!! Then I threw myself in the water. For two seconds, I thought that I was about to die.

As I was in the water, I remember hearing someone say, "Take her out". As I came out of the water, the deliverance began. On that day, God by the power of the Holy Spirit used the people at the noon day prayer to help me through to my deliverance. I saw Jesus. He came and he saved my soul. Later, God showed me ***Mark 3:20-30*** A house divided against itself cannot stand, So I had to come to the place of being sick and tired of being sick and tired to the point that I was ready to die to be with Jesus.

After God delivered me, he instructed me to fast. He kept speaking to me through Isaiah and Jeremiah. He was revealing things to me about the people in my life who were dealing with voodoo, black magic and witchcraft. It's not until he showed me this that I started to understand that a person can be born in to spiritual strongholds. But it is not until we give our life fully to Jesus Christ, who died for our sins that we may have life and that more abundantly. We can be delivered and set free from the strongholds in our life. When we are born into this world, we take after our mothers or fathers last name. That tells me that whatever our parents are carrying from their parents or ancestors will be transferred into the future generations. However when we come to Christ, he gives us a new life in him and destroys the yokes. We take after his nature as he transforms us. That means that my name may be Omie Garba but now I'm in Christ, I'm no longer attached to that name or associated to that name. He gave me a new name and that is Victory. I'm now in the kingdom of God where I have always belonged. In order to know the truth for myself, I had to go through the pain and the struggle to truly know Jesus as my Lord and Savior. In other words, I had to lose myself so that I can know and love him better.

It is now 2011 and I'm 25 years old. As I look at my life, I sometimes feel as If I have not accomplished anything and I know that is what the world says about me. I thought I would have a degree by this time and have seen the world, owning my own company and flying back and forth to Sweden. However I would not want anyone else's life because I have something that's priceless. I know Jesus who is the Love of my life, he is my every thing. No one and nothing can ever take Him from me. H's the one who saved my soul and set my spirit free to worship him. I am free to love him free to know him (John 8:36). We are all small and appear to be the same, but yet so different. As we grow older, our true beauty shows (like the butterfly). Like a butterfly, we are all different, and beautiful in our own way. In the Christian religion, the metamorphosis a butterfly undergoes is symbolic of the spiritual evolution all Christians go through. Butterflies represent rebirth and a new beginning. It is considered a soulful symbol. In ancient mythology, the butterfly stands for wisdom and everlasting knowledge Butterflies symbolize change. I know that Jesus is Lord. He is alive because he is the only one who is able to deliver, set free and destroy the works of the enemy. You may ask, how I can say that because he did that for me. He delivered me out of the hands of the enemy in a way that only he could. I was possessed and I did not know that I was, but Jesus knew and he set me free. No one wants to talk about this thing, because we have come to believe that when we come to Christ, everything is supposed to be as I call it, flower power. The truth is he is the one with the power. He overcame death. I'm a living testimony. Nothing can be too dead or broken in Jesus. Remember Jesus raised Lazurus from the dead, and he can do the same for you. It does not matter what it is, he can deliver and set you free, and nothing is too hard for Jesus Christ. To God be the glory!

A Woman of Courage

By Lady Elder Bessie

A Phenomenal Woman

A Woman of Courage stands guard in the doorway of her house protecting that which the enemy preys; with tears in her eyes and fear, worry, doubt, panic staring her in the face, she bows her head and begin to pray, Lord allow your huge outstretched arms to protect us and keep us perfectly safe,; Lord fend off all harm. We will fear nothing – not stray bullets in the night or evil spirits that walk in the day, because God in our refuge, He gives me strength to guard my house, Evil can't get close to us; harm can't get through the door because the Lord has ordered His angels to guard wherever we go; therefore we walk unharmed. Amen! Then she breathes in that breath of Strength, lifts her head and says I am a woman of courage not because fear, worry , doubt, terror and panic are not presence but because while in the presences of those; I am still standing guard of my house knowing God has strengthened me to stand strong for my house;

I Am A Woman of Courage – A Phenomenal Woman Standing Strong

MEMOIR XV

KIM'S MEMOIR
PUSH THROUGH THE PAIN

"He healeth the broken in heart, and bindeth up their wounds." Psalm 147:3 KJV

Imagine your mother betraying you and the Lord warning you because He loves you. The Lord sent a prophetess to a church in San Jose California in the eighties and she warned me to stop sharing intimate details about my life with my mother. How could this be? She was my mother who I adored and tried so hard to please but I failed miserably. I could not wrap my mind around my mom not being trustworthy and I disobeyed the Lord and I continued to confide in her for many painful years. I grew up in an abusive environment and I found myself being a victim for many years.

My father sexually and verbally abused me in my early childhood and he physically and verbally abused my mom and my adopted brother.

I have vivid images of the emotional abuse my father inflicted on us, he would display rages often by screaming and kicking doors down in our home. His veins would pop out of his neck as he shouted profanity and threatened to kill us. My mother would flee from the house by jumping into the white station wagon and driving fast to escape from being harmed. Can you imagine growing up in the most beautiful home in the neighborhood in a little town called East Palo Alto? Our house had fabulous accessories, a coffee table carved in wood with an artificial fish pond, antique end tables, decorative lamps, and an exquisite couch that was pleasing to the eye. It was like a museum because it definitely was the talk of the town and our family and friends were fascinated by the décor, but we could not move or enjoy the furniture because my father was obsessed with everything being perfect and in its exact location. I called my father (Freddie Cougar) because he was nightmare on Elm Street.

My mother finally had the strength to leave my father when I was ten and he continued to torment us after they separated because we lived in the house that he was obsessed with. When my parents divorced she was granted their home and we could not live in the house in peace. My mom sold the house and he repurchased the house and the abuse towards us diminished. When we visted him on the weekends I had to constantly hear how horrible my mother was and he lured us to his pity parties and he purchased blackmailing gifts.

My senior year in high school was extremely hard to deal with because the love of my life (my high school sweetheart) dumped me just before graduation and my mother kicked me out of the house. I was broken hearted and I did not know how to cope with the pain. I was told by my mother that I had to live with my biological father and I was terrified, but I had no other options so I was forced to live with him.

I lived with my father after graduating from high school and I reconciled with my high school sweetheart and my father hated him and threatened to do harm to him. I decided to have my own family that I could call my own and I deliberately got pregnant. . I hoped that my boyfriend would love me and the baby and marry me. Well I want to warn you that when you go outside of the will of God and you have you own plans it will cause you years of pain.
I wished that I had been strong enough to realize that my boyfriend did not have the capacity to love me.

I did not know how to seek the Lord for guidance nor did I ask Him if I was supposed to marry my husband and if it was ok to have children with him. The hatred I received from my husband's mom was unbearable. I hoped that his mom would like me because my parents were unable to nurture me and I was starving for love and attention. I was walking around with major pain and I had no idea how broken I was; yet I insisted on building a life with m husband. I was so dysfunctional I did not realize how I would harm my children emotionally and spiritually. I was not equipped to deal with life's challenges and nurture my children the way they needed to be nurtured. I was unable to be affectionate and talk to them as they were growing up. I had emotional breakdowns and verbal outbursts because I tried to bury the pain with shopping and sex.

Sixteen years I exposed myself to misery by holding on to a man who was emotionally and physically unavailable and my innocent kids had to experience neglect from both parents because of my unhealthy choices.

I did not know how to communicate effectively until I met a psychologist and joined TOASTMASTERS. We began to dig into the roots of my rage, hostility, abandonment, rejection, fear, anger, hatred, low self-esteem and passive aggressive behavior. Finally I had a voice and I was not judged; nor did my psychologist call me crazy even if I was. He began to coach me by role playing and he taught me how to identify abusive behavior because I did not know how to guard myself from bullies and predators.

Please realize that it takes the Spirit of God and therapy to expose predators and bullies. It takes time, prayer and fasting to pull down strongholds in our lives. I have experienced many strongholds in my life because I was exposed to some destructive spirits as I was growing up in an unhealthy environment.

Children learn what they live [Russ Berrie & Company, Inc]
If a child lives with criticism, He learns to condemn.

If a child lives with hostility, He learns to fight.
If a child lives with ridicule, He learns to be shy.
If a child lives with shame, He learns to feel guilty.
If a child lives with tolerance, He learns to be patient.
If a child lives with encouragement, He learns confidence.
If a child lives with praise, He learns to appreciate.
If a child lives with fairness, He learns justice.
If a child lives with security, He learns to have faith.
If a child lives with approval, He learns to like himself.
If a child lives with acceptance and friendship, He learns to find love in the world.

For many years I failed at restoring my relationship with my daughter and I did not know how to ease her pain. Many times I displayed passive aggressive behavior and I did not know how to give our unhealthy relationship completely to the Lord and I neglected to pray therefore fear sabotaged any chances of restoration. I asked her for forgiveness and for many years she refused to forgive me because she did not trust me.

I remember being so proud of her gifts and talents and I would pass out her business cards to promote her and she would be mean and unprofessional and would not make a commitment to serve the clients I would send her. I asked her why did she continue to lash out at me and be disrespectful and she told me that I was trying to take the credit for her creativity and talents when I had nothing to do with her being gifted. I felt like a knife had been placed in my heart and I realized that my daughter did not like me. I vowed to never send her any clients because I feared her getting pleasure out of punishing me by being hostile toward future clients.

I realized that the major pain between us is part of my journey and the Lord has to give me the strength to endure. I choose to walk in FORGIVENESS.

I am still pushing through the pain when dealing with my mother and daughter. Some days are enjoyable and some days are painful but I am privileged to know the Lord. I rely on the Lord to see me through the pain and I tell myself **to Push Through The Pain** because when you are in labor and the baby is scheduled for delivery you don't have the option to say "Oh I changed my mind; this is too painful" The Lord is allowing me to experience the good, the bad and the ugly. TGBTG (To God Be the Glory)

MEMOIR XVI

ELEANOR'S MEMOIR IN A SMALL TOWN

Create in me a clean heart, O God; and renew a right spirit within me. Cast me not away from thy presence; and take not thy holy spirit from me. Restore unto me the joy of thy salvation; and uphold me with thy free spirit. Psalm 51:10-12 KJV

Living in a small town, Moss Point, Mississippi, I could remember having some fun times; like in the summer time having bare foot relay races on the hot concrete to end of the block. That's as far as we were allowed to go. I remember listening to the crickets outside the window at night, or watching Sanford and Son or Flip Wilson with my grandfather, Leroy.

I was born on March 22, 1967 to Essie Taite 17 and Robert Biggs 18 in a small town in Alabama called Burnt Corn. I also could remember when the trouble began; it started at an early age. I was raised by my grandmother whom I love dearly. I was five years of age that I learned that I was living with my grandmother.

I was five years old when I learned what isolation and loneliness felt like. While my cousins had their moms and dads, I had neither. My mom lived in California with her new family; while my dad lived 20 miles across town also with his wife and family. Where was my family? Everyone had one except me. All I had was my grandmother, who worked all the time and had her own issues with an alcoholic husband. My grandmother was a great provider, but she couldn't give me the attention and love I needed because of the issues that her husband had with alcohol. This would cause her to leave me with my Aunt Rea. I hated to go over her house because her husband would do inappropriate things to me. He would do things that I believe an uncle shouldn't do, touching me in places he shouldn't and having my cousin who was very younger than me help him. When you are five, you are supposed to feel secure and safe around the people who take care of you and love you. When you're five you are supposed to run and play with friends and enjoy being five years old. I never told anyone about my uncle, except the thirteen year old girl from across the street. I never said a word; not even to my mom when I went to live with her in California at the age of seven. Now, I am with my mother in this strange place with strange people. I came from one place of isolation and loneliness to another. My mom was a single parent, who worked long hours and my little sister would attend preschool and extended care. Why couldn't I go to extended care?

I was scared to be at home alone. I was seven I wasn't supposed to be by myself. Someone should have been taking care of me. As I got older, it seemed as if I was always alone, but I wasn't. God had a hedge of protection around me from a praying grandmother. Being alone caused me to eat and rebel. As a result of the eating, I became over weight.

This caused me to become angry, because the children would tease me and would not play with me in school. Once again, I was isolated and alone. But, I wasn't really alone, for the One who gave me life was there. Even though my life seemed grim because of so much mistrust, I found solace in the gift God gave me, my fifth grade teacher, Mrs. Bivens. She would allow me to sing to the class in our free time.

Singing opened the doors for me to play clarinet and violin in the school band; thanks, to Mrs. Bivens. God allowed her to see something in an outcast little fat girl. I went on to King Estates Jr. High. The first years were great until I had a fight and got expelled. I had to spend my ninth grade year at Frick Jr. High. I had to leave all my friends and meet new ones; unsure of how they would react toward me. It went fine, because God already had it designed and set up in his plan.

I graduated and went to Castlemont High. In my sophomore year I met this young man, Danny McCrary. This is when my life took a shift. My grades went plummeting downhill. I started cutting school. Then the ultimate happened. Little Ms. Eleanor is pregnant at 15. OMG (Oh My Goodness) this was not supposed to happen. I was supposed to graduate high school, go to college and become a lawyer.

My mom was so upset when we received the results. Her exact words were, "You are going to get it when we get home." I was so scared! I just knew I was going to get beat. She didn't do anything. She gave me bus fare and lunch money and told me to go to school; she would deal with me later. The fight began when I was told that I was not keeping the baby. Every one talked to me and explained that I was too young to have a baby. After thinking long and hard, I realized that I was too young. It was a hard decision because I didn't want to get rid of my baby. But, I did it to keep peace with my mom. My high school years then took a spiral turn; once again I started cutting classes. I missed so much school that I was placed in truancy. Then I was being expelled once again. I was sent to a continuation school, Rudsdale Continuation. Even though this school was half a day, I still wouldn't go. I was now placed in home study, where once a week I go to class to turn in my homework for the month. This had my mom very upset with me. It got to the point where she wasn't speaking to me. This hurt because I felt I had disappointed her, so I tried to fix the situation by getting a job. It was official I was considered a total DROPOUT. I did a get a job. I got hired through JTPA, which had a contract with Naval Air Station, in Alameda. I was hired as a student aide, in the Human Resource Dept. I was very excited; I thought getting a job would ease the tension in the house. It didn't. She wasn't as upset, because I had a job at 17. Things seemed to be coming together until I met Herbert Joyner from Sobrante Park, he was 22. He was nice and bought me nice things. Before I knew it, I started missing work; because I was spending more time with Herbert. This angered my mom. She put me out. I was homeless at 18 living with Herbert in Sobrante. A few weeks later I find out I was pregnant. What a way to disappoint my parent who worked very hard to provide for me and my sister. How do I repay her by becoming a dropout with a baby? Well she wasn't pleased, but there wasn't anything she could do, because I was 18. Eventually, she accepted that I was pregnant. I moved back home when the house caught fire and Herbert went to jail for a violation. The months went by so quickly, before I knew it, I was in labor. My baby was coming down the birth canal rear end first. I had to have an emergency caesarean.

On March 16, 1986, I gave birth to a 6lb 13oz baby girl. I named her Hyniya Savannah Felise. She was born French breach; which means her legs were folded toward her face. She was a pretty little girl. We stayed with my mom until she was 4 weeks old, and we moved into Herbert's mother's (Shirley) apartment on East 33rd off of 13th Avenue, with my cousin as roommates.

On May 1, 1986, is when my life felt like it took a turn for the worse. On this day, I lost my eight week old daughter to SIDS. Some of my cousins were saying, I killed my daughter; that I rolled over on her and smothered her. I couldn't understand why God was allowing me to go through this; I was only 19. I asked why God took my daughter. My Aunt told me not to question God. She said, "You're young. He will bless you with another child. It wasn't until I established a relationship with God to know that I couldn't question him.

I learned that He allowed us to go through certain situations so that we may encourage someone else. He also allowed me to go through the abuse of being beat by my deceased daughter's dad, so that I would tell some young women how God brought me out and turned that situation around. Herbert later apologized for the things he did and we became good friends before he got killed.

My aunt was right. God did bless me with not one, but two. I was pregnant with twins. I was not happy! I cried! How was I supposed to take care of two babies? This pregnancy was stressful; the twin's father was verbally and physically abusive. I was kidnapped at 4 ½ months of my pregnancy. He held me against my will because I didn't want to be with him. My mom had to call the police and send them to where I was, because he wouldn't let me go. Of course a few weeks later, I went back. He was so apologetic; I wanted to believe he was sincere.

That lasted for a few months. He didn't like the clothes I was wearing or my hair. I didn't have a lot of maternity clothes, so I wore some of my old pants and put a rubber band through the button loops and a big shirt. He didn't like this; so he cut my clothes off of me. He cut my hair because he said that I looked like this female he used to date. What a way to be treated while you are pregnant! This was supposed to be a joyous moment. I was a nervous wreck. This situation put the twins in distress.

I was only 28 weeks when I gave birth to twin girls, Tyreka Alanza and Tyiesha Alandra, weighing 2lbs 2 oz and 2lbs and 4oz. I could hold them with one hand. They stayed in the hospital until they weighted 6lbs.

They were sent home with heart monitors. I was too young for this. But God gave me the strength to manage. It wasn't until three months later that I found out that one of the twins had Downs's syndrome (Tyiesha).

How was I going to deal with this? But their doctor told me Tyreka would stimulate and teach Tyiesha. And she did, even though she was delayed a few months, she still learned her body parts, her ABC's and how to count from 1 to 10, right along with her sister. The only problem was she couldn't walk. This was because of her hearing, which made her equilibrium off balance. After the ENT (ear, nose, and throat) specialist surgically placed tiny hearing tubes in her ears, she began to walk. How excited I was! Tyiesha was now right with her sister in growth. She could say her nickname which was Be Be. Everything seemed to be good; the twins were getting big and exploring more. Then tragedy hits once again, Tyiesha had a fever, I tried everything to break the fever of 104. When calling the doctor's office I was told to give her Tylenol and plenty of fluids.

Tyiesha wasn't lying around or whiny, but I knew something was seriously wrong because she kept trying to take the pain out of her mouth and she kept falling. The last time she fell, she couldn't get up, I took her to Children's hospital, and the doctors ordered a lot of tests. My 2 yr old daughter was very sick; she had pneumonia and had suffered a febrile stroke! I didn't know that it was God revealing to me that my daughter had suffered a stroke. I knew before the doctors told me. The twin's father who was in jail received the news from his sister. He called cursing and saying, I was an unfit mother. He said, I let her get sick. It was explained to him that it was unpreventable. Down's syndrome children always have upper respiratory problems, which cause them to always have runny noses. So NO, it wasn't my fault!

Tyeisha stayed in the hospital 5 months. She was released a day before her 3rd birthday. She could no longer walk. She couldn't feed herself. She only had use of her right arm, and she suffered from seizures. I was too young to be dealing with this. I do believe that my grandmother had prayers stored up for me, for what was to come next. God gave me strength to deal with my daughter, whose little eyes would light up every time she would see my face; especially when she came in from school. Her smiling and saying hi, gave me strength, as well as hope.

My little family and I did well for three years. At age six, Tyiesha got sick again. Once again, she had a runny nose and a fever. This time, I didn't call the doctor's office. We went directly to Children's Hospital. The ER doctor sent us home, saying it was viral infection, meaning it was only a cold. My instruction was to give her some Tylenol and Triaminic cough syrup. We were discharged after being there for 4 hrs for the doctor to say that. We got home, I fed them both, gave them their baths, did as I was instructed and put them to bed.

The next morning I woke up at 6:30am to get Tyreka ready for school. As I entered the room, Tyiesha was still asleep. After giving Tyreka her clothes, I went into the kitchen to prepare Tyreka's breakfast.

Tyreka ate her breakfast, she went into the room to get coat. As she got her coat she gave Tyiesha a kiss and said bye Be Be. Tyiesha open her eyes smiled and went back to sleep, I thought. My fiancé of 6 yrs was there with Tyiesha. I went and dropped Tyreka off at school. When I returned home, I went directly to the kid's room to check on Tyiesha. I noticed that her eyes were half open and she sounded like she was snoring. So I went closer and shook her and called her name. I repeated this several times. She was non-responsive, so I picked her up. Her body went limp. I called out to Jermaine, he ran in the room. I told him, Be Be won't wake up. So I called 911. The fire department and paramedics came together. I explained what happened and that she was just at Children's Hospital and they sent her home stating that it was an upper viral infection. They tried to wake her up, but she was non-responsive. She was breathing (shallow breathing). They had to incubate her. As they placed the breathing tube in her mouth down to the appropriate area, she coughed and out of the tube came brown mucus. She was taken to Eden Hospital where she was pronounced dead on arrival. Not again! I was devastated. How was I going to explain to Re Re that her sister was dead? The ER doctor asked if I wanted to say good bye to Tyiesha. I told the doctor, No! I was angry because the hospital had sent her home to die. I didn't get angry at God. I felt like he was trying to get my attention, but like Jonah I was running.

Later that evening, I received a phone call from the twin's father from San Quentin. He asked, what happened. I explained. He never once asked how I was. He just started cursing me out and telling me I was an unfit mother. He said I let his daughter die. He said, I was too busy messing with my fiancé and wasn't paying attention that she was sick.

Oh my goodness, I had to plan another funeral. I couldn't do this; not again. My fiancé's mom and my mom made the arrangements. My sister Shawnyette got her dressed and the twin's cousin, Sha Sha combed her hair. I couldn't do it, I didn't have enough strength. I dressed Hyniya.

The funeral was nice, but very emotional for every one that Tyiesha touched, especially Alisha because she gave her the nickname and discovered her top teeth cutting through. She said, "They looked like butter beans." The funeral was disrupted by Champ's family when they arrived. They were 30 minutes into Pastor Stewart's eulogy trying to set up a video camera to record the funeral for Champ. My fiancé and I was furious! Are you serious?! I went from being furious to being embarrassed by their conduct. After the funeral we proceeded to Rolling Hills where the drama truly begins. Marguerite, Champ's sister carried on so bad, cursing and making provocative accusation about Champ and myself, that Pastor Stewart stopped the procession of the funeral.

She was really disrespecting my daughter (her niece's) funeral, as well as me and my family. The Lord humbled me and bridled my tongue through the insults and her calling me out of my name. It wasn't anything but the hand of God holding me back and my mom saying, "Faye don't listen to that. Let's go." We made it through that drama, but it was the talk of the year.

I am so glad that God gives us a measure of humor. I can now look back at that nonsense and chuckle. Praise God for creating us in his image! The rumors started, Tyiesha died of AIDS. So then I was angry all over again. Where do people get this stuff? If my twins tested positive for HIV, I think I would've been the first to know. This rumor started from someone who knew Champ tested positive for HIV. But I wasn't going to believe anyone else. I was going to ask the source. Well, I asked and of course, he denied it. It wasn't until years later when went to San Quentin that I found out the truth. He got very sick and was transported to Highland Hospital. He was diagnosed with Cryptococcus Meningitis. The meningitis made his legs numb; he had to take certain medication to help with the numbness. It wasn't until he asked for AZT, one of the first HIV/AIDS drugs, that I knew for sure he was positive, because this wasn't a regular drug. My heart dropped! I thought Oh my goodness, its true. I asked his sister how long she knew he was positive. She stated, 15 months. He denied he was positive to the very end. He died in May 1997.

Little girls when they're young dream of fairytale romances. Like romances with a prince charming and a castle with a chariot and white horses those are the dream of little girls. Oh and don't forget the glass slippers. Little girls today dream of their junior proms and senior balls. Those dreams were shattered and now gone for me, because I am now a number. I am a woman living with HIV. My prince charming was my kid's father someone whom I trusted and thought I loved. I went through the pain of bearing his children (twins) to now bearing the pain of taking medication for the rest of my life. I thought he loved his kids and me, but the only thing he cared about was his cars, money and seeing me whenever he wanted to have sex.

Being young and naïve, I continued to have unprotected sex with him, because he was the father of my kids. I didn't believe that my prince charming would bring me any diseases, but he did. He brought me HIV. Something in a million years, I wouldn't think or believe I'd get. But I did. When I got my diagnosis, I was in shock. I was living with HIV for a long time, if I hadn't gotten tested when I did, I would've died.

This is another chapter to add to the book of my life. It wasn't until I got saved that I realized that God kept me while I was walking around with this disease. Like that song I used to hear the elder's singing, "I could've been dead sleeping in my grave but God told death to behave." Now, I truly understand that part of the song, because I am a living witness. Praise God!

If I had been tested earlier, it would've prevented my kidney disease. Late detection allowed the virus to attack my kidneys. I thought Oh my goodness, kidney failure, dialysis? What is dialysis? Bring in shock with my results of HIV, but I was devastated, denial should've been the appropriate word. I wasn't accepting that diagnosis! I adjusted well to HIV; it's been 14 years as of July 13, 2011, Praise God!

God gave me the strength to deal with the HIV as well as transition into a new life in him. Kidney failure was difficult. After being on dialysis for 8 years, I am still adjusting. I don't like sitting for 3 hours. If I could've asked God to let me choose my illness, I wouldn't have chosen this. I didn't know that the kidneys help with the major functions of the body: like regulating the blood pressure, removing waste products from the bloodstream, etc. Even though I don't like the fact that I have to come to dialysis three times a week, I thank God for his favor of second, third, fourth and fifth chances. He tried to get my attention with the death of both my children, the abuse from the fathers of my kids and HIV. It was then and only then that he had to sit me down, so that I could hear him, and that was through hemo-dialysis three times a week for three hours. God had my attention!

Often times we take the blessings God gives us for granted, like the kids I lost, I looked at it as, I'm young, I can have more. But when you loose a vital organ from kidney disease, liver disease, or heart disease, that's when God has your undivided attention. That's when you have to rely solely on him (grace and mercy) and stand on his promises (his word). The Bible says in Isaiah 53:5, *"But he was wounded for our transgressions, he was bruised for out iniquities: the chastisement of our peace was upon him; and with his stripes we are healed.* So I started believing in my heart that I would be healed, some day; if not here on earth in this life then I will be with him in eternal life!

MEMOIR XVII

INEZY'S MEMOIR
REBORN TO BE

Strength and honour are her clothing; and she shall rejoice in time to come. She openeth her mouth with wisdom; and in her tongue is the law of kindness. Proverbs 31:25-26 KJV

I was raised in a single parent household. My mother was very strict and she sheltered me. My mother worked in the Berkeley School district for 35 years.

As a little girl, I was a dreamer and had my own mind that wanted attention from men. I can remember them saying I was a pretty little Barbie doll. I hated being labeled as a mixed child. I only wanted to be black; I didn't want to be pretty. I wanted love from men not for being pretty but for what I could offer on the inside.

I was raised in the Church and taught to believe in God. But I felt empty and looked for love and affection. When I reached the age of 12 years old, I got pregnant and aborted the baby. By this time I was drinking, smoking marijuana, taking prescription pills and was soon introduced to what was then known as free basing (now known as smoking crack).

At this time my boyfriend was 21 years old and I thought I was in love at the age of 14 years old, but I was actually looking and seeking for a Father figure. I soon became pregnant and decided to keep the baby. I remained in this relationship for 7 years; which consisted of physical, verbal, emotional, financial and sexual abuse. I was isolated and not allowed to have any friends so he transported me to and from school. He was jealous and insecure to the point that he would frequently check my underwear and do his own personal pap smear to make sure that I had not cheated on him. By this time I was addiction to drugs, stealing and being a thug. I was in and out of juvenile for various crimes. My mother was hurt and tried her best to help me in every way that she could but I was just lost and turned out.

When I reached the age of 18 years old I tried a different relationship and soon became pregnant with my second child. This man was a drug dealer and deep sea diver (liked to perform oral sex). He was worse than my first relationship in regards to his abusive behavior toward me. He would call me horrible names, pistol whip me, sleep with other women and gave me so many STD's until I lost count.

He did not allow me to eat pork. He would beat me with baseball bats on my legs. By the time I was 5 months pregnant with my second child, I begin smoking crack. When he found out, he took me one night and tied me up with duct tape. Then he threw onion bits, hot sauce and vodka all over my body and beat me for 4 hours with a heavy dog chain. I just knew he was going to kill me that night. Then he made me get in a bathtub filled with milk then to the bed to have sex with him.

The beatings continued and he told me that if I ever left him, he would kill me and my little girl. Eventually I was able to get out of this relationship because I started seeing a gang member of whom he was afraid. When I finally left, he kept our daughter (my second daughter) stated that if I tried to take her, he would hurt my family.

By this time I was a full blown addict and started working the streets and selling my body for drugs. It was during this time that I met what was to be my third daughter's father. He was abusive to me and his hustle was pick pocketing and women. There were 4 of us living together and sharing him. We moved from state to state pick pocketing and forging checks. I went to prison over and over all the while lying to my family regarding my well-being. My last prison term for check forgery was 5 years, 5 months and 3 days.

Once I was released from prison, I continued my life of crime, lying to my children, mother and family promising them that I was going to get some help. I was now the mother of 4 girls of which the last was delivered during my prison term. From the age of 14 – 42 years old my mother cared for and raised my girls.

By now, I hated all men and felt that the only thing they could offer me was money. I then began experimenting with heroin, mixing it with crack to shoot into my veins. I had always vowed that I would never use heroin. You have to be careful in what you say.

I became so low in my addiction that I begin selling my body for as little as $10 for the drugs.

At the age of 42, upon my last and final prison release, I asked God to give me the courage to change. However, I got off that prison bus and celebrated by drinking and smoking marijuana. The next day I felt dumb and knew I had made a mistake. I realized that this old lifestyle did not feel right. I then truly surrendered to God, gave everything to Him and no longer desired to play games, or hurt others.
I strongly desired my family to trust me and wanted an opportunity to be an active mother and grandmother.

I am here to tell you that my entire life has been restored. I repented of the awful things I had done to my family and others, and forgave myself as well. My heart is now full of love today and I have a personal relationship with God.

After 30 years of bondage and suffering, I am finally free of addictions and pursuing my educational goals one day at a time. I finally have my woman's worth, walking with my head up. I have been reborn to be me.

I can look in the mirror every morning and see the good work of God. And you can see how powerful the Lord is. I can truly say today I love myself. I'm here to tell you I finally got my Woman's worth. I share my story because I have no more shame or guilt and would like to give hope to every woman that's been in bondage.

I have a calling and passion to help other women and young girls that are still out there in bondage. I want to help millions of ladies to break the chains. I know that there is someone that can relate to my story. So, I'm here to tell you that God can and will RESTORE you.

I am continuously reaching for the love of my Lord and Savior because although I left Him, He never left me alone. Today, I can truly say that I have an awesome relationship with God. And when you see me, you can see the light. If you keep the faith and fully surrender you will see His power.

I must say that it is a blessing and an honor to be me again. Thank you Jesus, I love you with all my heart.

ABOUT THE AUTHOR

Lady Elder Bessie Sims is a multi-talented teacher, speaker, contributing writer to Victorious Living for Moms, and life coach. Her voice and prophetic anointing are used by God to blow the trumpet to end-time believers so they may hear the clarion call of God across the nation. Anointed with a true apostolic and prophetic call her desire is to leave an imprint on every life she comes in contact with by encouraging them to come into the knowledge of the power that worketh in them to do exceeding, abundantly above all they can ask or think.

Her mandate from the Lord is to travel the breadth of this country to preach, teach, motivate and build the Body of Christ with revelation, prophetic insight, wisdom, knowledge and help the people of God to return to their first love through prayer and true worship. God's powerful fivefold anointing is evidence as she ministers the word with power and authority. Restoration, deliverance and miracles are signs of the power of God in her ministry.

She is a visionary called and commissioned by the Lord to empower woman and help them discover who they are. As a result of this commission Lady Elder Sims has launch into ministry for the furtherance of the Gospel. The first ministry is Millennium Ministries for Christ, Inc. which allows her to go out into the hedges and byway all across this land preach the Good news about Jesus Christ. To go into home and pray for the sick, visit women shelters and teach bible studies, have girl talk and make-up and Tea Parties to help the women with self-esteem and confidence. Millennium Ministries feeds the homeless, provide blankets and clothing for those in need.

Under the mantle of Millennium Ministry is Women of Worship (W.O.W.) is a Bible-teaching worship seminar, classes, teleconferences designed specifically to encourage, equip, empower, and engage women to live a life of true worship. These events are structured to help catapult women into Bible study, prayer, evangelism, corporate worship, and a full life of true worship. W.O.W. understands that "Worship, in its total essence, is a RESPONSE TO TRUTH." Therefore, in every session, the Word of God is presented with clarity to given the women the opportunity and the choice to respond to Truth which is in essence real worship. W.O.W. is unique in that way to provide BIBLE TEACHING WORSHIP EVENT such as Women of Worship One Day Conferences, Blog Talk Radio Show to teach the Word of God and every 1st and 3rd Friday of the month at 5 am PST we have prayer.

The other ministry is Phenomenal Woman Empowerment Alliance, Inc. PWEA focus on inspiring, encouraging and empowering women to understand their worth, the power within, their passion and purpose for life to become the Phenomenal Woman the meant to be! The PWEA is dedicated to challenging women from all walks of life and socioeconomic platforms to embrace their God given passion and purpose, cultivate their talent, and become a phenomenal leader in every area of their life! PWEA accomplishes this mission by focusing on education, mentorship and coaching, and collaboration of women seeking to advance in leadership, start or grow their own business. PWEA is an organization that characterizes value, passion, and purpose, and focuses on networking, empowerment and the advancement of women from all walks of life. And through the support of the community and different organization, PWEA provides and looking to provide more programs and initiatives for women seeking to improve their lives and circumstances. The dynamic collaboration of energy and talent provide the foundation and support required to deliver the prospect of economic empowerment and advancement of women. WE ARE PHENOMENAL WOMEN DOING A PHENOMENAL WORK!!

Lady Elder Bessie Sims stands by the side of her husband Pastor Jonathan Sims as he has been lead by the Lord to out into ministry. Pastor Sims is the founder of New Hope Worship Center in Richmond, CA. Before launching into ministry Lady Sims was an integral member of Covenant Worship Center in Berkeley, CA under the Leadership of Lead Pastor, District K. R. Woods and she serves with her husband as Care Pastor, Executive Board Members, Outreach Pastors and New Member Administrator. She also serves on the District Board of Directors of the Pentecostal Assemblies of the World District #3 as Communications Liaison Secretary to District #3. She is also a member of (R)ELIEF Elect Ladies International Empowerment Fellowship serving as Communication Liaison Director under the Leadership of First Lady Crisette Ellis.

Lady Elder Bessie Sims is a mother of five beautiful daughters – three who are contributing poets in the book Victorious Living for Moms: Letters to a Mother's Heart. She is the wife of Pastor Jonathan Sims!!

I Am A Woman Phenomenally!!

I defied the odds;

I soar above life's issues

I made my enemy my footstool;

I allowed wisdom and grace to lead me and now I walk in Victory!

Now God can use me to make a real impact in the lives of others!

I Am A Woman, Phenomenally!!

www.ingramcontent.com/pod-product-compliance
Lightning Source LLC
Chambersburg PA
CBHW052111090426
42741CB00009B/1761

* 9 7 8 1 9 3 6 8 6 7 0 2 8 *